SECRETS
OF
WINNING
SLOTS

ABOUT THE AUTHOR

Avery Cardoza is the foremost gambling authority in the world and best-selling author of twenty-one gambling books and advanced strategies, including the encyclopedic *How to Win at Gambling*, and the best selling classic, *Winning Casino Blackjack for the Non-Counter*.

Cardoza began his gambling career underage in Las Vegas as a professional blackjack player beating the casinos at their own game and was soon barred from one casino after another. In 1981, when even the biggest casinos refused him play, he founded Cardoza Publishing, which has sold more than seven million books and published more than 100 gaming titles.

Though originally from Brooklyn, New York, where he is occasionally found, Cardoza has used his winnings to pursue a lifestyle of extensive travelling which has included extended sojourns in exotic locales around the world. And of course, Las Vegas, where he did extensive research into the mathematical, emotional and psychological aspects of winning.

In 1994, he established Cardoza Entertainment, a multimedia development and publishing house, to produce interactive gambling simulations that give players a taste of a real casino; not only with animated and responsive dealers, but with the full scale of bets at the proper odds. The result, *Avery Cardoza's Casino*, featuring 65 gambling variations, became an instant entertainment best-seller making its way onto USA Today's best-seller's list.

Cardoza's most recent project is *Avery Cardoza's Player*, a new and exciting gambling lifestyle magazine that celebrates the fun, the energy, and the pleasures of casino gaming at its best. Every issue of *Player* features writing from the top gambling authorities in the world—the names you know and have come to trust. Check it out at www.cardozaplayer.com.

SECRETS OF WINNING SLOTS

Avery Cardoza

CARDOZA PUBLISHING

ABOUT THE PUBLISHER

Cardoza Publishing is the foremost gaming and gambling publisher in the world with a library of over 100 up-to-date and easy-to-read books and strategies. These authoritative works are written by the top experts in their fields and with more than five million books in print, represent the best-selling and most popular gaming books anywhere.

SECOND EDITION

Copyright ©1998, 2003 by Avery Cardoza
- All Rights Reserved -

Library of Congress Catalog No: 2003109493
ISBN: 1-58042-117-2

Write for your free catalogue of gaming and gambling books, advanced strategies and computer games.

CARDOZA PUBLISHING

P.O. Box 1500, Cooper Station, New York, NY 10276
Phone (800) 577-WINS
www.cardozapub.com

TABLE OF CONTENTS

STRATEGY CHARTS

THE BASICS OF SLOTS

Introduction

I'm going to show you how to beat the casinos at slots, and in the process, how to get free rooms, free comp buffets, free meals, free line passes to move you ahead of other patrons in long lines, discounted or free tickets to the best shows in town, and much more.

This book will show you how to live like a king; playing the slots, drinking for free, and doing all the other pleasurable things you do in Vegas and in your other favorite gambling locales — all on the house. Sounds too good to be true? In this book, I'll give you the key to unlocking all the freebies you can handle.

This book is about winning and having a great time at the casinos while giving yourself the best chances of beating the slots. Can it be done? Of course, but only if you know how to put the odds on your side. There are many misconceptions among players; I'm going to dispel these and focus on how to work the machines in your favor.

You'll learn how to find the best machines, how to guarantee that winning sessions remain winning sessions, how to minimize losing sessions, how to find the machines paying the highest returns and how to avoid ones that attract suckers like sitting ducks. Once you know how to get all the freebies that the casinos have to offer, you may have earned yourself a free vacation doing exactly what you like to do — playing slots!

A Little Advice

The temptation of playing for monster jackpots combined with the allure of gambling has turned the slot machine business into a multi-billion dollar industry. Walking through a casino and seeing the mania surrounding endless banks of machines is simply awe-inspiring for the first time visitor. After all, who can believe the noise and excitement of the hordes of slots players revelling in the machines?

Welcome to Las Vegas, Atlantic City, the riverboats, and the endless other venues where the slots are king. No longer are the slot machines just a noisy profit center for the casinos. They now generate more than 50% of the average casino's income, and in some casinos, whose sole gambling game is the slots (known as slots palaces), they make up a full 100% of the income.

Interestingly, one major difference between slots players and other casino-goers is that the slots players generally play their machines without too many illusions. They play for fun with no serious expectations of winning. The game is relaxing for them, especially fun when winning, but the bottom line is they know the casino's got the edge and will probably take some of their money. Just the same though, they can have good time.

Many other gamblers — the players who take on the table games — know that the casinos have an edge, but still believe somehow that they're going to beat the odds. Some of these gamblers are even convinced that they're going to win. Paycheck after paycheck goes into these beliefs, the casinos build more spectacular facades and larger towers, more mega-resorts get constructed every year with upwards of 4,000 rooms to feast on gamblers, and yet, the dream of the dreamers still doesn't fade.

Slots players seem to be more realistic in their whole approach. Their dream of hitting the big one is tempered by the fact that they know the casino is going to win, ultimately. But if they get lucky, and the reels line up in their favor, oh, that could be sweet.

The goal of this book is to educate you, not only about the slot machines in all their aspects, but also about the realities of gambling. Misconceptions abound, and I want to remove these from your understanding so that you approach the machines sanely, with cold hard facts on your side, all illusions scattered to the winds.

Let's start with the basics. Gambling is about risking money, and in a casino, with few exceptions, the odds are against you. This means that you should have the expectation of losing money when you play. You also have the possibilities of winning, and the slim possibilities of winning very, very big. But the fact remains: if you gamble long enough, you will probably lose. The law of odds says so; every enormous casino built on losers' money says so; empirical evidence says so. And what's more, deep down, when sanity rears it's wizened eyes, every gambler knows it.

The slot machines you play in the casinos have been set so that mathematically, they will show a profit to the casino. I will show you techniques and strategies to bring those odds down to the bare minimum, and money management strategies that will allow you to win sometimes, but the raw fact is that your expectation is to lose money in the long run. There is no way around it. Not every slots player will lose, for luck shows winners sometimes, but just about everyone who plays for any length of time will be ground down by the odds, and will lose money.

So the need here is to play sanely with a full understanding of what you can and can't do. The goal is to bring the odds down to the bare minimum, and when winning, to take the money as profits. The higher goal is to put yourself in the position to have fun also, and that means to bet within your means so no possible run of bad luck can really hurt you, financially or emotionally. I will talk a lot about money management in this book, because there is nothing more important to the gambler.

Fortunately for the slots player, there are ways to cash in on the casino's eagerness to draw you in, and this leads to good things, such as free meals, shows, rooms, giveaways, cash rebates, and more. I'll show you how to take advantage of being a slots player

Let's move on now and see if we can't find out more about the slots.

History of the Slot Machine

Introduction

The development of the slots industry and its first machine dates back about 100 colorful years, and got its start on the West Coast of the United States. Everything gets its start somewhere, and in the case of slots, it all began with one man.

Charles August Fey, a German immigrant who settled in San Francisco in the late nineteenth century, is credited with the invention of the slot machine as we know it today, with spinning reels and cash payoffs. Inspired by Gustav Schultze's poker gaming devices of the 1890's which were found mainly in saloons and paid only cigars and free drinks, Fey devised a mechanical device in 1899 built of cast iron, called the Liberty Bell.

Fey's original machine set precedent for the entire line of future slots, with three reels containing symbols such as liberty bells, horseshoes, and stars. The term "Bell" soon became the universal reference to all three-reel slot machines. The highest payoff was a set of three liberty bells. Following is the payout chart for this original.

1899 Fey Liberty Bell Payout Chart

<u>Symbols</u>	<u># of Trade Checks</u>
Three bells	20
Flush of hearts	16
Flush of diamonds	12
Flush of spades	8
Two horseshoes/One star	4
Two horseshoes	2

Other machines at the time had playing card suits, with three reels, ten symbols per reel. In 1901, Fey's first Draw Poker machine offered two plays for each nickel deposited, with an opportunity to win cigars for different card combinations. For example, fifty cigars for a royal flush, ten cigars for four aces, and two cigars for three queens. With pressure from players who wanted cash rewards, Fey eventually converted his machines to cash paying games, making them the first three reel slot machines to offer coin payouts.

Payout Chart for Fey's Poker Slot Machine

Combination	Free Cigars
Royal Flush	50
Straight Flush	20
Four aces	10
Four kings	8
Four queens	7
Four under queens	5
Full hand	4
Flush	3
Straight	3
Three aces	3
Three kings	3
Three queens	2
Three under queens	2
Two pair aces up	2
Under aces	1
Two aces	1

Referred to as "drop card machines," a large number of earlier poker machines possessed only fifty playing cards, usually omitting the ten of spades and the jack of hearts. Without these two cards, the chance of getting a Royal Flush was reduced dramatically. The games accepted nickels for play, and the cards were attached to spinning drums that would flip them when the handle was pulled.

The Beginning of Mass Production

Fey made deals with saloon owners to place slots in their businesses, with an agreement to split the profits 50/50. At this time, machines sat directly on bar tops, and returned 86% of coins, with a 14% profit left to be divided between Fey and the saloon owner. Originally, Fey worked from his basement, building the games by hand, and servicing the machines by horse and buggy, until he could no longer keep up with the construction of the machines alone. In 1896, Fey opened a factory at 406 Market Street in San Francisco to meet the increasing demands from business owners.

Of course, with any popular invention comes a rush of anxious businessmen looking for a way to get their piece of the pie. One such businessman was Herbert Stephen Mills, an entrepreneur and successful manufacturer of various carnival games. Inspired by Fey's machines, Mills began mass producing his own line of slots, mimicking them after the original Liberty Bell.

In 1906, The Mills Novelty Company of Chicago was established, producing the Mills Liberty Bell, High Top and Golden Falls. These games became popular immediately, and were soon sold across the country to saloons, bowling alleys, pool parlors, and other businesses.

Around the same period of time, other manufacturers began producing large, free-standing, ornate wheel machines, which became the most popular cash slots for a period of time. The actual wheel resembled the wheel found on the modern-day television show Wheel of Fortune, with the exception of denominations printed on the various colors. Fifty to one hundred colorful strips were found on the larger models. Players would select which color they wanted to play by depositing their coin into the desired slot. They would then pull a lever on the left side of the machine, waiting anxiously to see if the arrow would land on their chosen color.

The Mills Company produced the first popular floor machine, called the Kalamazoo. This game gave players the option to insert one to five coins at a time, and paid up to $1. When wheel machines proved to be successful, other manufacturers immediately began to produce their own versions of the original model while adding minor improvements. For example, Caille-Schiemer Co. produced the first six coin game called The Puck, while the Mills Co. remained in the running with the first ten coin game, The Duplex.

The Klondike, manufactured by Fey was a smaller version of the wheel machines, and sat directly on bar tops. The wheel exhibited six different colors; red, white, black, blue, yellow and green. A glass window at the front of the machine displayed the chosen color. Players could deposit up to six coins for their chance to win up to twenty-five drinks. The yellow strip paid twelve drinks, blue paid six, white three, green two, and red and black only one.

Fey's Klondike Payout Chart	
Color	**Free Drinks**
Yellow	12
Blue	6
White	3
Green	2
Red	1
Black	1

The Roaring '20s

By 1927, the Mills Novelty Company became one of the nation's largest factories, employing over 1,000 people. There are many reasons for Mill's rapid success. He not only boosted sales through lowering prices, mail-order catalogues, and increased advertising, but also by making the games more aesthetically pleasing to the player. The Mills machines had a glass window in the front of the game so that the player could actually see the monetary award waiting to gush out to the lucky winner.

Players were also able to see three rows of symbols, which let the player see just how close he had actually come to winning. Within forty years, over a half million Mills slot machines had been sold.

The prosperity during the Roaring Twenties led nickel machines to evolve into dime, quarter and half dollar machines. Because people were willing to play with larger denominations of money, manufacturers raced to produce and convert games that would accept larger sums.

Caille Brothers developed the Superior Jackpot Bell in 1928, while Fey invented the Silver Dollar, the first Bell machine to allow players a chance to deposit a coin of that size.

1929 Silver Dollar Payout Chart - 5¢ machine

Combination	Payout
Three Bars	20
Three Bells	16
Two Bells/One Bar	16
Three Plums	12
Two Plums/One Bar	12
Three Oranges	8
Two Oranges/One Bar	8
Two Cherries/One Lemon	4
Two Cherries/One Bell	4
Two Cherries	2

The 1920s also marked the beginning of jackpot displays, allowing players to see large amounts of money waiting to be won. The coins were visible through one or two windows positioned in the front of the machine. During this time cast iron machines were converted to aluminum machines as well.

Within just thirty years of Fey's invention, over a million slot machines had been manufactured worldwide. Slot machines had started to become very serious business.

The '30s, '40s, and '50s

1931 through 1941 marked the "Golden Age of Slots." Prohibition gave rise to the notorious speakeasies — illegal hangouts that served alcohol and housed slot machines. The sale of slots soared during this period, with an annual revenue of approximately $150 million. Although politicians and law enforcement agencies fought against the slot machines, they continued to increase in popularity. Even during the Depression, hopeful players flocked to the machines for a chance to hit the jackpot.

In 1935, Watling Manufacturing introduced the ROL-A-TOR, a slot machine that showed the last nine coins deposited through a large rotary devise at the top of the game. The name changed to ROL-A-TOP the following year, and in no time almost every manufacturer had their own version of this type of game.

During the 1940s World War II was raging, which affected the manufacturing of slots. Many slot machine facilities converted to war production manufacturing plants. Shortages of aluminum caused slot machine manufacturers to return to cast iron designs. In 1942, the manufacturing of slot machines stopped completely until the war ended.

The end of the 1940s and the beginning of the 1950s produced a unique type of attention-getting slot machines. Frank Polk, a reputable artist, created a line of carved wooden statues to encase slot machines such as the Mills High-Tops. The figures were intricate, life-like designs in the form of cowboys, Indians, miners, and other western figures. Like many of the other earlier machines, these unique slot machines are collector's items and have a whole legion of enthusiasts collecting, trading, buying and selling these vintage goodies.

The '60s & '70s
The Electromechanical Era

In the 1960s Bally's Manufacturing, which had concentrated on arcade machines and other coin-operated devises since the 1930s, began to successfully design and produce slot machines. Their machines were unique in that they utilized electro-mechanical circuitry to recognize a large number of payout possibilities. They also replaced the single-coin slicer of earlier machines with a hopper payout devise.

Bally's 1963 Money Honey machine possessed an ingenious hopper unit that was able to contain 2,500 dimes. Left-to-right and right-to-left payouts as well as five-line machines are credited to these innovations. Bally's accomplishments of the 1960s pushed them to the forefront of manufacturing throughout the next decade. Bally's controlled 90% of the slot machine market in Nevada during the 1970s, and also profited by sales abroad to countries that permitted gambling.

In 1967, a significant development in design came with the production of Bally's famous "809," the first slot machine to give players an option to play more than one coin at a time while getting proportional winning payouts for the additional coins. The 809 allowed up to five coin play. Each additional coin deposited in the machine increased the payout amount.

Casinos that had originally scoffed at this new idea soon saw it for what it was — a money maker that greatly increased a player's excitement and their bottom line.

Bally's 1967 809 Slot Machine				
Symbol	**1st Coin**	**2nd Coin**	**3rd Coin**	**4th Coin** **5th Coin**
3 Bars	$10	$20	$30	$40 $50
3 Melons	$7.50	$15	$22.50	$30 $37.50
3 Stars	$5	$10	$15	$20 $25

The '80s & '90s - The Computer Age

In the 1980's, Bally's manufactured a series of machines called the Series E. These omitted the electromechanical circuitry, and replaced it with the technologically superior microprocessor. These devices were more reliable than their predecessors and were easier to maintain. Around this same time, music chips were inserted in the microprocessor, adding to the appeal of the game. Passerby's were not only enticed by the attractive designs on the machines, but were also engaged by the new sounds that occurred when coins were inserted and the reels were spun.

Microprocessors, or "chips" controlled the entire workings of the machine; from the coin meters to the intricate symbols. Stored in the memory, chips contain information on how often the machine is played, the last time it paid out and the amount that it paid out. Microprocessors are the "brains" of today's slot machines.

Bally's 1983 E2088 - $1 Slot Machine

1st Coin
Cherry/Cherry = $5
Cherry = $1

2nd Coin
Bell/Bell/Bell or Bar = $20
Orange/Orange/Orange or Bar = $10

3rd Coin
3 Bars = $100

4th Coin
3 *$1,000 Symbols* = $1,000

While Bally's is still a major player in the slots market, they are no longer *the* player, that title belongs to IGT, International Game Technology. This Reno-based slot manufacturer dominates the industry. Many of the top earners among slot machines are manufactured by IGT, including their Double Diamond and Triple Diamond machines, their Red, White and Blue series, and their Sizzling Sevens and Wild Cherries machines. As the leader in the industry, IGT tries to maintain their footing with aggressive marketing and innovative design.

One new line that was introduced by IGT was their Wheel of Fortune design. This fun machine has payouts for various winning combinations, but the real excitement comes when you line up the three wheel of fortune symbols.

Then, the Wheel of Fortune above spins, with the possibilities of you winning anywhere from twenty-five all the way up to 1,000 times on their progressive.

The Evolution of Slots and the Future

Slot machines have come a long way from Fey's Liberty Bell. While some of the original concepts have remained — the reels, some of the symbols, and the coin acceptors — time has marched forward as well. From nickel-ante type machines paying out cigars, cigarettes, drinks, and modest winnings, the stakes and prizes have now become enormous. Chances to win cars, expensive prizes and millions of dollars, are now the lures. The slot machine craze that began with Charles Fey building machines in his basement exploded into a billion dollar industry.

Manufacturers have now added flashing lights, ringing bells and various attention-getting features to compete for the coins of hopeful players. Devices have been added for convenience; credit card and bill acceptors, buttons for rapid, easy play (in addition to the handles) and options to utilize accrued winnings instead of having to continuously insert money. Machines accept multiple coins for play, and progressives linked with banks of machines not only within a casino, but inter-casino have added a new dimension. There are also machines with multiple payout lines and with wild symbols.

The fundamentals of determining winning combinations has completely evolved as well. Keeping in time with the computer age, slot machines are micro-processor based, running on chips and sophisticated programs that track everything from time played and average bet, to number of combinations won and average yield over any number of variables. That's a long way from the strictly mechanical machines of the early days.

But as they say, the more things change, the more they stay the same. The slots are still the slots; players still like them, and still play them.

Whatever changes may come over the next 100 years, in all likelihood, gamblers will still be playing the slots. They may be activated then by handles, buttons, visual cues, or even brain waves. I can't see far enough ahead to know the methods, but I can see far enough behind to know they'll still be around, and players will still be playing them and trying to beat them.

Legal Milestones for Slots

Although a billion dollar industry today, slot machines had to endure many setbacks and bombardments throughout the years. On April 18, 1906, a tremendous earthquake rocked San Francisco and the surrounding area. The entire San Francisco slots manufacturing base was devastated. In no time, however, the industry bounced right back into business.

This natural disaster was interpreted by various religious groups as a sign from God concerning the sinfulness and evils of the slots-playing world. These groups fought to outlaw not only slot machines, but also liquor and saloons. With pressure from many different directions, slot machines were outlawed in San Francisco in 1909. Nevada followed in 1910, and the entire state of California in 1911. Soon many other states followed.

Manufacturers refused to become deterred by these new laws, so they decided to relocate to the East Coast. In 1912 Nevada legalized slots only as trade stimulators, with the stipulation that the machines could not pay out any monetary awards. Machines such as the Caille Gum Vendor, made by the Caille Brothers were produced to offer the players prizes like candy or gum. These types of machines enticed women and children to play, which was socially frowned upon, creating an immediate uproar. If a woman was seen chewing gum, people automatically assumed that she had been playing the slot machines, which led to the social taboo of gum-chewing for women.

One of the more popular trade simulators was the Liberty Bell Gum Fruit Model, produced in 1910. This was simply a typical slot machine with a gum vendor attached on the side to dispense winnings. The symbols represented the various flavors of the gum: spearmint, lemon, orange and plum. The slot machines of today continue to utilize the fruit symbols, and the original stick of gum symbol has evolved into the "bar" as we know it today. The lemon found on these machines actually gave rise to referring to malfunctioning cars as "lemons."

The battle against saloons and slot machines continued to be led by groups such as the Anti-Saloon League and the Women's Christian Temperance Union. These groups pressured the government, finally becoming victorious on August 1, 1917 when the Senate passed a resolution to create the 18th Amendment, which outlawed the manufacturing, distribution, sale and use of alcohol. On January 16, 1920, this became law.

With Prohibition came an enormous boom in the slots business with an ebbing in the popularity of the gum-vending machines. During Prohibition, the majority of the speakeasies relied on slot machines for up to 20% of their profits.

A break for slot manufacturers came in 1931 when Nevada legalized gambling. Drinking was then legalized in 1933, but slots remained illegal in the other states. In 1934, New York's Mayor LaGuardia made an impact on the gambling world by hurling over 1,000 machines into the ocean. Orders were given to destroy any and all slot machines on the spot no matter what.

Slots manufacturers however, remained in business full throttle by building gambling ships in offshore waters equipped with slot machines and table games. The "Golden Age of Slots" came to an end during World War II due to the conversion of slots manufacturing factories into war production facilities. When the war ended, the demand for slot machines rose again immediately.

During the 1950's, the Strip in Las Vegas and the city of Reno began to thrive. In 1951, however, Congress passed the Johnson Act, which terminated all interstate slot machine shipping to enforce the laws against slots. While shipping continued to states that allowed such interstate commerce, it had a negative effect on business in the non-legal states.

This ban, to various degrees, continues even into the 90s, almost fifty years later. Most states allow the collection of slot machines for personal use (about eight don't allow slot machines of any type for any reason), but only according to varying legal definitions. Generally speaking, you're allowed to own slot machines if they are "antiques," which again, depending on the state, could be anything from ten to thirty years old, to machines manufactured only before 1941, as in South Dakota. You'll need to check on applicable laws before venturing into these waters.

In 1976, the slots manufacturers got a big boon when the state of New Jersey decided to allow machines in Atlantic City. Further boons came in the 80s and 90s as the Mississippi riverboat states followed suit, Indian reservations opened casinos nationwide, and manufacturers began heavily courting business in overseas markets.

While slot machines are not legal for gambling use in states everywhere, business is certainly booming, and the industry is healthy and growing. Imagine this: More than $100 billion dollars is wagered on slots every year in the United States alone. Yes, this is a big industry.

The Elements of a Slot Machine

Slot machines are composed of various functioning parts. It will help to be familiar with them. I'll go over them here.

The Machine

The Reels

The spinning mechanism on slot machines that contain symbols are the **reels,** technically known as **stepper reels** for the various "steps" or "stops." A typical slots machine will contain three reels, as the earliest machines did back when Fey invented them.

There are four reel machines in play today. Specialty machines, mostly novelty-type slots, have as many as ten reels, and are often referred to as *Big Berthas.*

Each reel on a slot machine contains a number of **steps** or **stops**, places where the wheel can end when it is spun. This stop may contain a **symbol**, such as a cherry or lemon, or it may even contain a **blank**, a stop with no symbol.

Before slots with microcomputer chips were introduced, the typical reels contained twenty to twenty-four stops. Multiplying the typical three reel machine by twenty stops per reel gave the machines a total of 8,000 combinations: 20 x 20 x 20. Machines that used twenty-four reels offered a possibility for slots operators to determine their winning payouts according to a total number of 13,824 chances.

Of course, whether there were a total of 8,000 combinations or 13,824 combinations makes no difference to a player's winning chances. It is all determined by the likelihood of hitting winning combinations, and the amount that is awarded when they occur. Both of these factors are established by the slot manufacturer according to the purchaser's specifications.

Nowadays, with winning combinations determined by sophisticated programs that emulate random spins, reels contain as many as 128 stops, which gives manufacturers much greater flexibility in setting and adjusting the payout schedules and frequency of hits they'll offer to the players. The typical 128 stop machine contains twenty-two actual symbols and 106 blanks.

On this new generation of microchip machines, the concept of a stop differs from the electromechanical and earlier predecessors in that the "stop" is no longer necessarily a physical place where the reel stopped, but a *simulated* place. There was no need to create 106 blank stops using a computer chip. Rather, the program would simulate a wheel containing 106 blanks to go along with the twenty-two symbols. The frequency of hits and number of payouts would be set by the program designer, and that total combination of possibilities, as set by the manufacturer, would determine the percentage payout that might be expected by the player. To loosen or tighten the machine, all the casino has to do is replace the chip with a new one, and the deed is done.

The Payline

The glass window in front of a slot machine's reels is marked by a horizontal line, called a **payline**. Winning combinations must line up directly behind this line for the spin to be a paying winner. That's why it's called the *payline*. If winning symbols line up, but they're not directly behind the payline, then the spin is not a winner. All winning spins in slots must appear behind the payline.

Some machines have three or five paylines. When there are three paylines, they will generally be lined up as three horizontals, one in the middle, and one each above and below that line. Usually, it takes one coin for each payline to be activated. Machines with five paylines usually add two diagonal paylines. These slots need the full five coins for all paylines to be active.

The Payout Display

On the top of each slot machine is a **payout display** with a colorful attractive design listing all the winning combinations that can be spun and the number of coins or absolute dollar amount that will be paid when there is a winner. Other special winning combinations or conditions are printed here as well.

The payout display will show the winning payouts for every coin played, and if the machine is a progressive, will either show the progressive total on the machine itself, or be marked "Progressive." When "Progressive" is indicated on the payout display, that jackpot total will be prominently displayed on a large display sign above the bank of progressive machines.

Service Light/Candle Light

On top of each slot machine is a red indicator light, known as the **Service Light**, or **Candle Light**, which will light up whenever the services of a slots employee is needed. The red light will be activated, or lit, when the player presses the CHANGE button requesting assistance, when the machine malfunctions, or when a jackpot is hit and the machine is unable to payout the full amount of coins. The last condition is the one I really like to see, that and all the noise that comes with it too.

The Coin Tray

On the bottom facing of each tray is a metal tray, called the **coin tray**. This is where the coins pour out of the new machines on winning combinations. Pushing the CASH OUT button causes the machine to disgorge it's full bevy of winnings. Bang! Bang! Bang!

The Slots Handle

Pulling on the slots handle, a long handle located on the right side of slot machines, will spin the reels, provided of course that coins are deposited into the machine or credits have been played. (No bet, no play.) Using the handle is the traditional way of spinning the reels and playing slots, and is still preferred by many players, even with the advent of the easier credit buttons. We'll see how long they remain since play by the credit button is easier and probably the playing style of choice for modern players.

While the result of pulling the slots handle is exactly the same as when it was first created almost 100 years ago, there is a major difference in its actual functionality. Originally, pulling the handle would mechanically set the reels in motion. Now, it does no such thing. Slot machines are microchip units and not mechanically triggered. Pulling the handle on modern machines activates the software, which sets the reels in motion — a quantum difference from the pre-80's machines.

The Play Buttons

In this section, I describe the active play buttons you might find on a slots machine. Note that some of the buttons listed may have slightly different names, depending on the manufacturer, but in general, they serve the same function.

Spin Reels

When coins are inserted into the machine, or less than the full amount of credits are played, you will have to manually press the SPIN REELS button to spin the reels and get the action going. (You can also pull the slots handle.)

Play Max Credits/Bet Max Coins

Pressing the PLAY MAX CREDITS button will play the full amount of credits allowed on the machine and automatically spin the reels. Thus, if the machine accepts five coins as a bet, pressing PLAY MAX CREDITS will deduct five coins from your credits. Similarly, if three coins were the maximum bet, then three coins would be played and that amount would be deducted.

This button may also read as BET MAX COINS or PLAY ALL CREDITS, or may have another similar designation which would amount to the same thing. The PLAY MAX CREDITS button will only activate the reels (and deduct the coins played) if money is in the credit. If there is no credit accrued in the machine, you will have to insert more money into the heart of the beast, and play off of that until credits are reestablished.

Play Two Credits, Play Three Credits

On some machines that accept two coins or three coins, you may see a button that states PLAY TWO COINS or PLAY THREE COINS. These would serve the same function as the PLAY MAX CREDITS button. For example, if you saw PLAY TWO COINS on a machine, that machine would most likely accept two coins as the maximum bet. Pressing the button would deduct two from your credits and spin the reels. These buttons also may read as BET TWO COINS, PLAY TWO CREDITS, BET THREE COINS, or PLAY THREE CREDITS.

Play One Credit

For players who prefer playing one credit at a time, the slots have a "PLAY ONE CREDIT" button on every machine. Pressing this button will play one credit toward the next pull. Note: this will not automatically activate the reels as the PLAY MAX CREDITS button does.

However, nothing will happen, that is, the reels will not spin until the handle is pulled or the SPIN REELS button is pressed.

You can also pay two credits by pressing the "Play One Credit" button twice, or three coins by pressing it three times, or the maximum number of credits by pressing this button until the full allowance of coins is reached.

This button may also read as BET ONE COIN or PLAY ONE CREDIT, or have another similar designation amounting to the same thing.

The Cash Out Button

The CASH OUT button, when pressed, converts all the credits built up over the playing session into coins that drop like a metal waterfall into the coin drop below.

Players use the CASH OUT button, located prominently on the front of the machine, when they're ready to change machines, to call it a day at the machines altogether, or simply to hear the victory charge of coins pounding into the coin drop. The sound of coins dropping is always fun!

The Change Button

On the far left position on the button display will be a CHANGE button. This convenient button brings you door to door service from the changeperson. (Normally *changegirl*, but males do occupy these formerly all-female jobs in some casinos now.) Pressing the CHANGE button lights up the red candle light at the top of your machine and lets the attendants know that you need service.

I actually have a quick story about the change button. On my last trip to Las Vegas, I was interviewing the slots manager at a small off-strip casino while seated at one of the slots. I was on a stool, leaning with my back against the machine, facing the slots manager who stood behind me. He was busy explaining his knowledge of the slots, which, just as typical of casino employees as with players, was rife with misconceptions.

In the middle of the conversation, a changeperson came by, interrupted the manager's conversation with a half sarcastic, half joking remark, reached over me to hit a button on the machine, and moved on again. I thought that he was play-acting a spin of the reels and thought nothing of it. The conversation continued with the same scenario repeating itself a few minutes later, and then a third time after that. I couldn't figure out why the changeperson kept interrupting his manager.

It was only later, while I was studying the machine's design, I think it was an IGT *Red, White and Blue,* that I realized I had been leaning on the change button, and the changeperson came hurriedly over each time to find his services weren't needed. So that's what was going on. Anyway, those change buttons do work.

The Displays

There will be several displays on the front of the machine. While different slots may display the information in different locations, and include things others won't, the basic information will remain the same and be part of any modern slot machine.

Credits Played or Coins Played

The **Credits Played** display shows how many coins are being bet on this particular spin. This display may also be listed as **Coins Played**. Thus, if three coins are played, the display would indicate the number "3" for your information.

Credits

The **Credits** indicator shows how many credits you have accumulated either through winning spins, or through money entered into the machine. Each credit shown will reflect the denomination of coin you're playing.

For example, placing a $20 bill into a 25¢ machine will enter eighty 25¢ credits into your account. The indicator in Credits will read "80." If you play three credits, the Credits will read "77." If that spin is a win for twenty credits, the Credits will read "97" to reflect the twenty coins win. If that $20 was entered in a dollar machine, then twenty credits (20) would be entered, or "400" on a 5¢ machine.

Playing the PLAY ONE CREDIT or PLAY ALL CREDITS button will automatically deduct those credits from your bankroll.

You can use your credits by either playing them through until the total is down to 0, (which means you've lost them all!), or hitting the CASH OUT button, which will convert credit into actual coins and send them noisily tumbling into the coin well.

Winner Paid

The **Winner Paid** indicator displays the amount won on the current spin. For example, if three liberty bells align for a winning combination paying forty coins, the Winner Paid display will read "40."

Insert Coin

When the machine is awaiting a play, the **Insert Coin** message will be lit. This lets the player know that he or she will need to drop some action into the machine to initiate play.

Error Code

Yet another indicator on the front of the machine is the error code indicator. Should the machine malfunction in some fashion, the error code indicator will display a code number that alerts the technician to the nature of the problem so he can address it and fix your machine. You won't typically see this in action since it will only light up when there is a problem.

The Symbols

Remarkably, many of the slot machine symbols have survived since they were first popularized back in the early part of the Twentieth century. The Liberty Bell symbol, found on the original Fey slots machine of 1899, can still be found on machines today!

What stands out among successful slot machines is the simplicity of the symbols. Cherries, lemons, sevens, liberty bells — all basic symbols familiar to slots players — have struck a chord over time. These basic symbols have long histories dating back more than fifty years, and somehow continue to hold strong even in today's modern slot machines.

Another prevalent symbol in the modern machines is the bar. Machines often feature bars in various forms: single bars, double bars, and triple bars.

There are many more symbols as well nowadays, especially with the large proliferation of slots machine manufacturers and machines that are made for current trends. In addition to the basic symbols discussed above, there are symbols galore to be found, from other fruits, numbers, and styles of bars, to a wide variety of "theme" machines with endless symbols created by designers ever eager to hit a machine that catches hold of enough players to be successful. But the most successful machines always come back to the basic symbols.

Wild Symbols

Wild symbols are becoming the latest trend in current designs. Certain machines will designate a particular symbol as "wild," which means that the wild symbol can be used as any symbol on the machine to create a winning combination. For example, BAR BAR Wild, would give you a payout for three bars, and LEMON Wild LEMON, and 7 7 Wild would give you winning combinations, to be paid according to the payout schedule on the front of the machine.

Some machines use the wild symbols to multiply the player's payout line. For example, on IGT's Double Diamond machine, the diamond symbol, when lined up to form a winning combination, will double the payout. Two diamonds are even better, they will double each other for four times the payout.

The Any Bar

A popular payout on slot machines is the *Any Bar* symbol. This means that any bar shown can be used in combination with any of the other bars to create a winner.

Blanks

In addition to the printed symbols on the slots machine are other stops, or blanks, which are simply blank spaces on the reel and have no winning potential.

The Basics of Play

Playing a slot machine is quite easy. It is no more complicated than putting coins in the machine itself, and either pulling the handle or pressing the "SPIN REELS" button. As the machines have become more sophisticated throughout the years, additional features have been added to make playing slots even easier.

This chapter will cover all the basics of play and general information you need to know to get set up at the machines, and to use the various features available. Let's start by understanding what you're trying to do.

Object of the Game

The goal in slots is to get the symbols on the reels to line up directly behind the payline in one of the winning combinations listed on the front of the machine. The higher ranked the combination, as listed, the greater the payout will be.

For some players, the real goal in slots is to hit the jackpot paying thousands of dollars, tens of thousands of dollars, or even millions of dollars on the big progressives. The particular goal at a machine, at least the big goal, is a function of the machine itself. Machines have a variety of jackpot sizes and rewards, but whatever the machine, you'd like to hit the big one.

All right, let's face it. The real goal for many of you is to hit paydirt: one pull, and it's off to Hawaii for a year or more as the first stop on your post-retirement trans-world luxury cruise; the ability to do whatever you want, whenever you want, without answering to the bossman anymore. Not a bad goal.

Exchanging Money
Getting Coins

The only thing easier than getting your bills changed into coins in Las Vegas is actually playing the machines once you've got them. The typical slots area gives you all sorts of ways, one easier than the next, to get coins for the machine you want to play.

First, you can go directly to a **change booth** set up in or near the slots area. Or, you can track down one of the many changepeople who patrol the machines, wheeling carts full of change. They usually aren't hard to spot. If that is too taxing, let them come to you. Either wait (they won't be long), or press the CHANGE button located on the left side of your machine. That will light up the red bulb atop your machine and alert changepeople to come with money.

You can also get change from the machine itself. The new machines have bill changers that accept $1, $5, $20, $50 and even $100 bills. These bills are converted directly into credits on the machine. Later, you can convert these to coins if you want, by pressing the CASH OUT button on the machine.

Coin Denominations

Slot machines come in a variety of coin denominations. You can play the **small coin** machines, 5¢, 10¢, and 25¢, the **medium** coin machines, 50¢ or $1, or the **big coin** machines, $5, $25, and $100 slots! You saw it right. There are $100 coin machines out there and they do get action!

The most popular machines played are the 25¢ and $1 machines, though where available, the 5¢ slots get good action as well. The big coin machines are found only in the larger casinos, while the 10¢ and 50¢ machines are not as readily found.

Converting Coins into Dollars

When you've finished playing and are ready to convert your coins into bills, you'll need to make your way over to the change booth that's set up in the slots area. There are wonderful machines in the booth that automatically sort and count your coins. The changeperson within simply takes your bucket, empties it upside down over the machine, and abracadabra! A few seconds later, the machine has counted up your total. That amount will be paid back to you by the changeperson in whatever denominations you please.

Note that the cashier's cage in the back is not typically set up to change coins, and they will just refer you back to the change booth in the slots area. If there is not a change booth, then the cashier's cage will serve as both the cage and the change booth.

Playing the Machines
Playing by Coin

Most players get going on the slot machines in the time-honored way of dropping coins directly into the machine, a method that hasn't changed from the original pre-slots designs more than a hundred years ago.

On every slot machine is a coin slot, called a **coin entry**, or **coin acceptor**. The coin entry is where you insert your coins into the machine to initiate action. Machines are set up to take varying amount of coins, depending upon the design. There are machines that take only one or two coins, others that accept up to three coins, and even others that take up to five coins per play. For example, a machine that plays three coins will accept either one, two, or three coins of action, and a machine that plays five coins, will accept one, two, three, four or five coins of action.

If you try to put more coins in the machine than it accepts, it will immediately return the extra coins into the coin tray. For example, if four coins are placed into a three coin machine, the extra coin will drop out the bottom, to be returned to the player.

Newer designs don't limit themselves to five coins. There are already six coin machines in the casinos, and newer models, like IGT's Black Rhino, that accept up to forty-five coins. This is just the beginning. In the not too distant future, I imagine that a new breed of slot machines won't even accept coins; they'll be playable only from a special slots card or credit card that contains credits for play.

The physical aspect of handling coins and the noise they make when hitting the metal coin well are a distinct part of the thrill of the game itself, but in time, I imagine that too will give way to the march of the computer age. People will eventually look back at the current coin machines, much as we look back at mechanical slots, and see a relic of days gone past.

THE NEW SLOT MACHINES
Putting coins into a slot machine is fast becoming a relic of the past. While there are machines that can still be played by

coins, the new models being manufactured for the US market will take only paper money. You read that right. Many modern machines cannot be played by coins! But that's not the only change brought by modernization of the industry.

The old term for slot machines, "one armed bandits," so named because the reels were activated by the handle on the side of the machine, is no longer appropriate. For one, most players don't even use the handles anymore – that is, if the machine even has a handle! A simple press of the button does everything.

For another, where the reels stop is not a mechanical function, as before, but is calculated by computer chips using random number generators. The function of the mechanical device that spins the reels now is only to *display* the result calculated by the computer, not to *determine* it.

In fact, the modern day slot machine is essentially a fancied up computer device. We have come a long way, baby.

Establishing Credits

There are two ways to establish credits at a machine. The basic way of building credits is by simply putting coins or bills in the machine. Once your money is in, you can play. With bill acceptors inserted into the latest versions of machines, you can immediately establish credits by inserting a $20 or $100 into the machine. These credits will register on the display of the machine marked "Credits."

The second way is to earn these credits through wins. After every win, the amount won is automatically credited to your total. This amount will be posted underneath the area marked "credits" on the machine.

For example, if you line up a combination that pays eighteen coins, the number "18" will be posted for your credits. If you already had fifty credits accrued, then the win of eighteen would be added to that total for a new total of sixty-eight.

You can play on these credits as long as you have them, or cash out at any time by pressing the "CASH OUT" button.

Pressing the CASH OUT button will release the coins into the drop slot below. When there are a lot of coins won, the resultant noise will be a loud thunder of coins dropping, a commotion sure to raise the excitement level of all players within earshot of this winning hullabaloo.

If more coins are won than the machine will pay out, an attendant will come by to pay the rest, or get a manager to authorize that payment. Usually, the maximum amount of coins that the machine will pay for winners is posted right on the machine itself. It will also state that the attendant will pay the remainder. If that is the case, do not leave your machine if you hit a big winner - always wait until the attendant arrives to give you your winnings.

Tip

Never, ever leave a machine that owes you money. Wait for the attendants to come by no matter how long it takes. You should as soon leave your wallet on a New York City street corner as walk away from a machine that's stacked with winning credits.

The Slots Handle

The traditional way of playing slots is to use the handle located at the side of the machine to spin the reels. The original idea of the handle, besides it's basic function of being a method of spinning the reels, was to give players the feeling of controlling their destiny. There was action involved on the part of the player, and it was fun. Players felt like they participated, though in reality, for the average player, there was no skill involved in the way a handle was pulled. One pull was as good as any other.

I say "for the average player," because the casinos had their hands full with slots cheats who were able to control the destiny of the spins by using various methods and skills they had developed to manipulate results. Techniques such as slamming, walking the reels, and other methods were part of the slots cheat's arsenal. Slot machines today are caught between the new and the old. The reels can be activated by either pulling the handle, or pressing a button on the machine. Casinos prefer that players use the faster method of playing by button (and by credits), since it generates more dollars played per hour and higher profits. With both slots handle and button at their disposal, the style of play used is at the players discretion.

Experienced slots players tend to use the button more than the handle. They want the fast action and easy play of the buttons, especially since they camp out at their machines for hours at a time. Tourists and casual players, on the other hand, lean more toward the handle. These players are in no rush and they enjoy the physical participation. Slots, to them, usually means pulling the handle.

Playing Multiple Machines

You'll often see fanatical slots players working two machine at a time. Really ambitious players may play three simultaneously. Now that's action! The advantage of playing multiple machines is that players get more action, and by getting more action and having two machines working for them, they will hit winners more frequently.

However, there is a disadvantage to playing multiple machines, as I will discuss later in the winning strategies chapter. I will refer you to that section for a full discussion, but for now, suffice it to say that playing multiple machines lowers your chances of being a winner. Additionally, more money is now at risk.

If, despite my advice, you still insist on playing two or more slots simultaneously, just make sure that the total action you give both machines fits into your overall bankroll limits.

THE SLOTS ENVIRONMENT

You walk into the casino, hot cash in hand, and say to yourself, "I come to gamble." The casino is buzzing with noise and excitement, a hum of voices gather and hang in the air, over by the craps table a Texan is screaming, *"Eighter from Decatur."* You don't understand craps anyway. The blackjack tables are quieter, but don't look inviting, and roulette just isn't your style.

Forget all that. You came to play slots. Here's what the slots environment looks and feels like:

The Slots Setting

In casinos, slot machines dominate more floor space than any other gambling game. The slot machines make so much money for the casinos and generate so much action that a casino owner would have to be shortsighted not to maximize the presence of these machines wherever possible. And really, how can you have a real casino without the general noise and ruckus created by the bells, tumbling coins, and screaming of jackpot winners?

Slot machines are grouped together in groups called **banks**. A bank of machines might consist of four machines grouped together in a squarish shape, with backs toward the middle, and fronts facing outward toward the players, or even in larger groups of eight, ten, fifteen, or even more machines, in circular or rectangular shapes.

Often, banks of machines are built around a platform manned by a slots attendant whose job is to give the players change when needed, and keep the customers happy and playing. These configurations are called **carousels**.

Within each bank there are a variety of machines. You may see four or more machines of the same type from the same manufacturer next to a few from another within the same bank, or even alternating machines with no particular pattern you can discern.

The placement of machines is decided by the slots director or manager, who makes these decisions based upon what they perceive to be the maximum effectiveness. Thus, it is quite normal to see a multitude of different styles within the same bank. A bank of slots will usually contain machines using the same coin denomination. It is unusual to see different denominations such as 25¢ and $1 machines mixed together within the same bank.

For example, one bank will contain nothing but 25¢ machines, while a neighboring carousel will be all $1 slots. This type of arrangement makes it easier for customers to identify the type of machine they want, first by finding machines with the coin amount they want to play, then by choosing the style of machine they prefer.

Also, players that wish to switch machines or play two machines or more at a time, can easily do so with the same coin value by remaining in the same bank.

Progressive slot machines are typically "banked" together in the same block, and at the equal coin value, so that the posted sign showing the progressive jackpot above the machines can refer to all the machines within the group. Banks of progressives are common in a casino and great draws for players looking to make a lot of whoopee from a little whoopee.

It is compelling for slots players, just as it is for lotto players, to go for the dream of the ultimate killing, the jackpot of all jackpots, the outside hope that drives slots players to the machines in droves, and keeps them playing. Slots players, as much as any other group, love the stories of the million and multi-million dollar winners. They can never hear enough of these get-rich-quick fantasies as they're always thinking that it could happen to them. And it could, if they get lucky.

Slot machines get ever more colorful, seemingly by the year. Brightly lit displays, garish colors, flashing lights, and rows of seated players clunking coins into the machines make up the visuals of a slots area. Add to this to the cacophony of sounds from the machines themselves, the occasional pouring out of coins into the metal coin tray, and the periodic commotion caused by a gleeful winner, and you have the slots area.

Chairs

Each slot machine in the casino has a chair in front of it, so that you can play the machines in comfort, even if you were to go for hours, which many of the players do.

Plastic Buckets

Throughout the slots area, between the machines, sometimes on top or at the ends of aisles, are plastic buckets. They look like small ice buckets emblazoned with the name and logo of the casino on them, but it's not cold cubes they're meant to hold. It's coins, buckets full of them.

These plastic buckets are widely used by slots players to hold their coins after cashing out from a machine, so that they can transport their haul over to the cashier's cage. You'll often see players scooping coins out of the coin well and shoveling them into their buckets prior to leaving the machine. Some players will use the buckets while they play, as a convenient way to hold multiple coins.

SLOTS EMPLOYEES

The casino has a number of staff devoted to the slots area, and I'll go over their functions next.

Changepeople

You can't help but notice the number of changepeople constantly on patrol through the slots area, even in smaller casinos. The main job of these employees is to provide ready coins or tokens — nickels, dimes, quarters, half-dollars, dollars, and larger denominations — for any player that needs them. A secondary job of these "front line" slots people is to keep the player happy, whether through commiseration with a losing streak, exchanging small talk, or giving hints that a player might request.

Casinos are well aware that a moment's hesitation in getting a customer his or her change could cause that player to get bored or annoyed and leave the area, so they keep the area well-stocked with changepeople. It is not unusual to see two or even three changepeople patrolling a slots section.

Changepeople who work in stationery positions in the carousels often double as cheerleaders. Believe me, when these change-people root for you, they are really rooting for you, because a happy winning player tends to tip, sometimes really well.

Waitpeople

Slots are supposed to be fun, and to make sure you agree with the casino on this issue, they keep you well stocked with drinks while you play. You have a full choice of drinks available, from coffee, tea, milk and sodas, to beer, wine, shots and mixed drinks. You can also request cigarettes if you're a smoker.

And all of this is without charge.

However, just like any place that serves drinks, it is customary to tip the server — more if you've ordered a bunch of drinks, or if a big time win has you feeling large.

Slots Hosts

Most major casinos, and many smaller ones, have hired an employee specifically assigned to take care of the slots players' needs. This employee, called the slots host, often works out of a booth set aside for the slots players. The booth may have a placard that says "Slots Host," or "Casino Host."

The slots host spends much of his or her time working with slots club members, issuing new cards and memberships, processing special requests, or dealing with issues that come up. His or her job is to take good care of the slots players and make sure that their experiences at the casino are as first rate as he or she can make them.

Tipping

Tips are known as *tokes* in the casino.

Tipping is an expected service in casinos, just as it is in the table games, and many other service industries. There are several employees you may want to tip. First of all, you have the waitpeople bringing you drinks. It is customary to tip them every time a drink or round of drinks is brought to you.

It is also customary at the machines to tip the changeperson, especially at a carousel, if you're winning big. For example, if you win several hundred dollars, or several thousand dollars, you may want to spread a little love around to the changepeople that have helped you. If you really get lucky and win the jackpot, you may want to spread a lot of love around.

However, if you're losing, or not doing anything special at the machines, you really don't need to be giving out gratuities to the changepeople. Tips need only be given by winners - you've already donated enough to the coffers. Tips usually won't be expected from losers, unless a changeperson has given you incredible service.

The Different Types of Machines

In this chapter, I'll describe the various types of slot machines available for play, from the older style single coin machines, to the multi-coin machines, multipliers, progressives, Big Berthas, Buy-Your-Play, and Wild Symbol machines.

Choosing a Machine

The first step in playing the slots is choosing the machine you wish to play. You'll find a multitude of slot machines in the casinos, of many different styles and from many different manufacturers.

Actually choosing the right machine, the one that you're most comfortable playing and best fits your needs, will probably be the only time that you'll need to make a decision. From there, the actual playing of the machines is mostly automatic.

Single Coin Machines

The **single coin** machines, soon to be a dying breed, used to be the only type of slots available to the player, that is, until the invention of the multiple coin machine. Now single coin machines are rarely found, being much less profitable for the casino than a machine which takes two, three, or even five times as many coins, and by the same token, being that much less exciting to the players.

It is unlikely that you will find any single coin machines in larger and newer casinos because they are stocked with the most modern of machines. Singe coin machines still survive in smaller, less modernized clubs. Single coin machines have that old-time feel and are fun to play for that reason. They're a little slower and clunkier than their modern cousins, and playing just one coin per spin will have your money going a little longer.

Multipliers

In 1967, Bally's introduced the 908 machine, the first slot machine to take multiple coins for play while giving winning turns increased proportional payouts for every coin played. These slots are known as **multipliers**. These innovative machines led the way to a new era in slots. They are a way for the casinos to encourage their patrons to put in many times more coins.

The typical machines accept from one to five coins, with an occasional six coin machine to be found. Soon, there will be machines that accept much larger numbers of coins for a single play - that is simply inevitable. The typical machines now, however, accept either two, three or five coins as the standard maximum play.

A multiplier works much like a single coin machine, except that each coin deposited into the machine pays that much more proportionately than a single coin. Thus, two coins will pay twice a single coin for the same winning combination, three coins will pay three times, and five coins will pay five times. For example, if hitting three cherries pays two coins when a single coin is bet, three coins would yield a payout of six coins.

Multipliers work proportionately on all wins, typically, except for the biggest jackpot payoff, where a win for all coins played is much larger than if just one or two coins were deposited. This is how casinos encourage players to bet the maximum number of coins into the machine.

Now, multiple coin slots (as opposed to one coin slots) are about all you'll find in modern casinos. While these machines still accept single coin play, the majority of players bet the maximum number of coins permitted. One reason is that they get more action and bigger payouts if they win. Another reason, which I'll go into in greater detail later on, is that the big payout can only be activated by having the full number of coins deposited.

The machines I discuss below are all multiple coin type machines.

Multiple Payline Machines

Much like bingo, the **multiple payline** machines give slots players multiple directions that can turn them into a winner. The single payline machine has one line across the machine that shows where the reels must line up for a winning combination to be paid. The multiple payline machine, on the other hand, has three or five lines, depending upon the machine, which gives players more winning positions on the reels.

On these machines, each coin inserted activates another payline. On a three payout line machine, there are three horizontal lines. One line goes right across the middle as in a single payout line machine, a second line is above, and the third line below. To the left of each line, the display will be marked something like *1st coin payline* for the center line, *2nd coin payline* for the top line, and *3rd coin payline* for the lower line. As each coin is inserted, the payline boxes light up indicating that they're in play.

The five coin payline machines have two additional lines that crisscross the payout area diagonally. Appropriately, these machines are referred to as **five line criss-cross** machines, or simply **criss-cross** machines. These machines have additional boxes indicating *4th coin payline* and *5th coin payline*. These two indicators will light up when the fourth and fifth coins are inserted.

Winning spins can now be formed in any of the five directions on the five line machine, or on the three horizontals on the three line machine.

Keep in mind that while there may be more ways to win with these new directions and lines, the overall chances of winning are no better or worse than any other slots machine. These odds are set by the casinos on a machine by machine basis. If the payback percentages are set higher, you'll have a better chance of winning, and if they are set lower, then your chances are worse.

Buy-Your-Pay Machines

These frustrating machines sometimes catch unwary players off guard and account for annoying headaches when a player, who has seemingly scored a winning combination, or even a jackpot, finds out that not enough coins have been played, and ends up winning nothing.

You can recognize the **buy-your-pays** by looking at the payout schedule on the face of the machine. They'll show the combinations of winners when one coin is played, a different group of winners when a second coin is played, and an additional group of winners for additional coins played on three and five coin buy-your-pays.

The buy-your-pay slots work on a different concept than the other machines you'll find. These machines have a single payout line and typically accept up to three or five coins. They will only pay on certain symbols *if* enough coins are played. For example, the first coin might only credit cherries as the winner, but if another winner is hit, such as the bars, or sevens, it won't pay because the requisite number of coins weren't inserted!

These machines are less prevalent now than before, but since they can still be found, you'll need to be on guard if you find yourself playing them.

Again, if playing buy-your-pay machines, *always* play the maximum number of coins.

Wild Play Machines

The latest craze in slot machines are the **wild play machines**. These fun machines give players a chance to double, triple or even quintuple (five times) their winning payout if a wild symbol lines up as part of their winning combination. And if two wild symbols line up as part of that combination, the winning payout will be multiplied by four times, nine times and twenty-five times respectively.

When three wild symbols show, they are their own winning combination and are not multiplied by each other as with two wild symbols. You'll see that condition listed on the front of the slots.

These new machines add a lot to the excitement of the game, especially when they are hit. It's always fun to watch a winning combination take off when a wild symbol or even two is hit.

IGT is leading the way with their very popular Double and Triple Diamond machines. The wild symbol on these machines is, of course, the diamond. These machines are the most popular slot machines in the industry. You might also see machines on the floor with a five times multiplier. New machines are being developed and marketed all the time so you'll have to keep your eyes open for other exciting concepts as well.

Progressives

Progressives feature a growing jackpot that increases each time a coin is inserted into a machine that is hooked up to the progressive. When the jackpot does hit, the lucky player wins the total accumulated in the jackpot. At the same time, the jackpot total will be reset to a predetermined total, ready to begin climbing again.

Progressive jackpots can be relatively high if they've gone a while without hitting, or relatively low if they have been hit recently.

Following are two special types of progressive machines.

Mega Progressive Machines

The progressive slot machines draw tremendous amounts of excitement among players. The dream of hitting a one million dollar jackpot with one pull of the handle gets players excited. However, a one million dollar jackpot is a "small" jackpot nowadays. As more players get into these linked progressives, the jackpots are now in the *millions*. Five million dollar jackpots, ten million dollar jackpots, and even bigger ones are being hit by lucky players now.

Megabucks and *Quartermania* are two inter-casino linked mega-progressives with enormous jackpots.

Multiple Progressives

A newer type of machine has appeared on the slots scene, and that is the multiple progressives. For example, the Cool Millions slots by CDS Gaming, a one payline machine, offers players a chance to win three types of progressives. The big progressive, which on one of the machines I saw was $500,067.95, is won by lining up the three *cool million* symbols on the payline. The next two progressives, in the three thousand range but of varying amounts, were won by lining up three sevens, one set of either red or blue. There were other payouts as well.

Big Berthas

The classic Big Bertha machines are gigantic slot machines of many reels, usually eight to ten, that are strategically placed by casinos near their front entrance to lure curious players in for a pull or two. These novelty machines are always a fun distraction for passerbys new to casinos.

While the payout percentage on Big Berthas isn't very high, and the machines are mostly played by tourists for a pull or two, it is enjoyable for first-timers to pull the handle on the largest breed of slot machine in the world.

Misconceptions about Playing Slots

Being around the gambling world so frequently, I hear so many outrageous beliefs, falsehoods and outright misconceptions from gamblers, slots players, and casino employees about how slots really work that this chapter was needed to set the record straight. I felt that I couldn't put this book on the shelves without carefully addressing these issues so that you know exactly where you stand on these issues as a slots player.

So much misinformation is passed around that players start to believe it. Unfortunately, there are not many good sources out there to put things right, so players have a hard time finding out what is real and what is fiction. The information in this chapter is *real*, you can bank on that.

The worst misconceptions of all come from the people whom you might least expect - the casino employees who man the slots areas. I have talked to slots managers, floorpersons, slots hosts, and changepeople, and not once did I hear fewer than two facts or ideas on slots from them that were wrong. I thought if the people you would expect to be savvy, the ones working the slots areas every day, don't know the real deal, how could my readers possibly know? From other slots players? Not quite.

So before I move on to the winning strategies of the next chapter, let me set the record straight on a number of points. Whatever you think you know about slot machines that was gathered by information from casino employees and other players, I beseech you to leave your mind open now to rethink things.

I've heard hundreds of myths regarding slots and gambling in general; following is just a sampling of some of the most common ones I've come across. *Here we go.*

Myth: Slot machines are the worst gamble at a casino.

There are plenty worse gambles in the casino. Take a stroll down to the keno lounge or wheel of fortune, make some of the high percentage bets at craps, make bonehead plays at blackjack, bet a parlay at the sports book. An average loose machine pays better than roulette and all the previous examples.

Next time a friend tells you how bad your odds are at the slots, hear a little more about what they play and the bets they make. You may be getting the better end of the bargain.

Myth: Pulling the handle a certain way will make you a winner.

Whether or not you pull the handle slowly, quickly, gently or roughly will not alter your probability of winning. Pushing the "spin reel" button as opposed to pulling the handle won't change your luck either. You win or lose depending upon how the luck goes, and the little twirls and shuffles you might do to get the winner going won't make a difference, not mathematically.

This doesn't mean we're not all a little superstitious and will try every move to get the machines to cooperate. What I mean is, don't catch me with my own moves at the machines, I may get embarrassed. If I think standing on one leg is bringing me winners, I may be hopping like a bird. The reality, however, is that the machine can't see, feel or sense me hopping. And if it did, it might not understand what I was doing anyway. If it could, the slots gods would be having a good laugh. Wouldn't stop me from hopping though.

You can hang on to the handle, and flip over the end, kiss the machine, shower it with cupcakes, whisper "cool beans" in its ear, or stare it down like a demon cockatrice. No matter what, the odds will be the odds.

Myth: A machine that just won shouldn't be played because it won't pay out again for the longest time.

Just because someone won at a machine five minutes earlier doesn't mean that you couldn't hit the jackpot again five minutes later. It is unlikely that you will hit the jackpot five minutes later, but no more unlikely than if you played the machine next to it, or the one across the street.

Slot machines have no such programming installed, and if they did, it would be considered cheating. No casino is dumb enough to risk being shutdown for this, and no casino needs to even consider this. The slots give them plenty of built-in profits.

Myth: A machine that hasn't paid out recently is ready to hit.

Some players scour the casinos looking for machines that have been played for a long period of time without paying out. They believe that because this particular machine hasn't recently hit, it is due for a substantial pay out. Again, the machines are set to be random for every pull of the handle. What occurred the previous play has no bearing on the current play.

If you feel a particular machine is ready to hit, and feel comfortable playing it, by all means, give it a whirl. Just realize that your chances of winning at this machine are no better or worse than a similar machine that may have hit the day before.

Myth: Slot machine managers know when certain machines are due to pay out.

If a slots manager knew a machine was about to spit out the sweet land of milk and honey, believe me, you wouldn't be the one playing that machine. You'd be watching his or her mother, spouse, or other family member camped out in front of it.

Myth: Machines pay less when a slots club card is in it.

A slots club card is issued by casinos to their guests for the specific reason of tracking a player's action and rewarding them for this action. Good players get an array of perks - comp passes or discounts to meals, shows, hotel rooms, priority bookings and service, cash rebates, and much more.

The notion that casinos have set the circuitry of the machines to pay less when a slots card is inserted is unfounded. Casinos would risk far too much with the gaming board to play this kind of game. They already have their profits built-in, and certainly don't want to make the machines less attractive for their premier players. If anything, the opposite might be true. Casinos have their slot machines set just the way they want them right now, slots card or not.

To reiterate, the sole purpose of the slots club card is to tally the amount spent by the gambler. This in no way alters the inner workings of the game to pay out less to the player. The card is used only as a tracking device of a player's action, nothing more.

Myth: Machines pay less during holidays and big events.

Casinos make enough profits from the slot machines without having to change their payout probabilities on holidays. Casinos want winners, because winning begets action. I know of no general policy at casinos that makes special provisions for changing payout percentages during crowded events.

You have to realize that Las Vegas, for example, is filled year-round with special events - boxing matches, large conventions, holidays, seasonal crowds, etc. If this myth were true, casinos would be so busy changing machine percentages that they would have a hard time getting anything else done.

Myth: Good machines are side by side.

If you're playing in a slots setting where the machines pay out poorly because they don't cater to serious slots players, then yes, this concept is true, since all the machines suck rocks. But if you're in a real casino where slots players go to play, then this is typically not the case.

As I said earlier, casinos mix up their good paying and bad paying machines so that with the good machines, there is a stereo effect of better paying machines mixed up in the slots areas. It is unlikely that you will find more than two hotties side by side. The typical mix, I think, puts a stinker next to a good one.

Myth: You will win more at the dollar machines.

You might lose more also. As I will discuss in great detail in *Money Management* chapter, the *average* higher denomination machines are set to pay at a higher percentage than the *average* lower denomination machines, but the few percentage points aren't worth it if that coin is over your head.

Hurrah, this is not entirely a myth, but you better read up on the money management discussions in this book before you bump up to bigger coins than you planned.

House Percentages on Slots

The unusual thing about slots, as opposed to all the other casino games, is that you never know the exact percentages you're facing at a particular slots machine. Nowhere on the machine are the odds posted, nor can you tell from the type of machine, the manufacturer, or where the machine sits, what the payback will be. Even the slots personnel working the floor don't know what these percentages are, or to what machines they apply.

You may see a casino advertise 98% or even 99% machines, but walk into the slots area and try to find those machines. There may be a few of them scattered around, but nowhere will there be a sign saying which machines they might be.

What do we know about payback percentages on the machines? First, let's go over just what is meant by "payback" and "house percentage." In this discussion, I'll be using both terms interchangeably. The *payback* is the amount the casino returns, on average, for every dollar placed into the machine. For example, if the casino advertises a 97% payback, they are telling you that for every hundred dollars invested into a machine, the expectation is that $97 of it will be returned.

In the long run, with hundreds of hours of plays, this is pretty much what will happen: the player will lose $3 on average for every $100 played. That's the long run expectation. This $3 is the *house percentage* or *house edge*. In gambling terms, it is also know as the casino's *vigorish* or *vig*.

In the short run, say a few hours or so of play, or even a dozen hours, anything can happen. Even though the casino has a vig of 3%, it wouldn't be unlikely for a player to be having a big day and be up hundreds on a quarter machine, or for some player to be hitting a jackpot worth thousands of dollars or much more. Even more likely, a player will be losing at the machine.

In other words, playing a machine with a 97% payback, your *expectation* is to lose $3 for every hundred dollars you gamble. This does not mean you *will* lose $3 for every hundred you bet. You may lose $20, or you may win $20. You may even hit the jackpot and be on easy street for the rest of your life. But in the long run, as many players challenge the machine, and hour upon hour is invested into the machine, the return percentage will most likely approximate 97%. That machine will get its $3 per hundred played.

When a player is playing against a house edge, it usually means he can expect to lose if enough hours are played.

The Actual House Percentages

The cut and dry fact at the slot machines is that the house has the advantage over the player, and the size of that advantage is strictly a function of the payback on the machines played. Paybacks on slots can vary from as little as 50% return on the dollar to as high, in rare cases, to 99+%. Taking into account the benefits you can earn from the strategies I'll discuss in the "Winning Strategy" and

"Slots Clubs" chapters, you can actually have the edge sometimes. However, the norm is that the casinos maintain an edge at slots, and build bigger ritzier casinos from that edge.

In Atlantic City, the minimum payback is regulated by the state regulatory board, which requires that the slot machines have no less than an 83% return on the dollar. In Nevada however, there are no minimum paybacks at all, and the casinos can set their machines at any percentage they want.

The Las Vegas casinos are in a very competitive market and compete heavily for patronage from the legions of slots players. This is good news for slots enthusiasts, because it makes for more competitive rates, which means a higher percentage payback. Most casinos set their machines for the mid-90% in payback. This is a high enough percentage to make a steady stream of money while at the same time allowing enough winners to keep everyone coming back for more.

Players react to ringing bells, flashing lights, clanging coins, and the whooping and hollering of winning players - all the signs that a slots player is winning. These casino sounds generate excitement throughout the immediate area and get everyone thinking about playing those machines. Everyone wants to win.

Casinos that set their machines in the mid 90% range generate a lot of these sounds, and thus a lot of play. That's why many of the Las Vegas casinos do so well at the slots. You'll find a lot of slots players, regular patrons and first timers, who get drawn into the slots action at good casinos. Excitement begets action. Within these casinos will be machines set at lower percentages for higher profit margins, but overall, the best way for casinos to make money is to make sure there are enough winners. That is why you'll find good and bad paying machines interspersed among one another.

There are also casinos in Las Vegas and elsewhere whose top machines will pay in the 80% range, perhaps lower. While these casinos will make a higher percentage of money per machine, they won't make anywhere near the gross amount of profit that a more savvy casino paying a higher percentage payback to the customer might make. Players realize quickly when they're at a machine that's not very encouraging. It doesn't take a rocket scientist to see that one is having less fun at a machine because of fewer payoffs.

Locals will migrate to where their luck is better and tourists will be more drawn to machines where the excitement level is higher. Sure, poorer paying machines will always have their customers, but not at the same intensity level or length of time played as in a casino that has set the mood for winning.

SLOTS CLUBS & WINNING STRATEGIES

Slots Clubs

The greatest boon to hit slots players yet, the slots clubs, are the best way for slots players to amass a seemingly endless parade of room comps, meal comps, show comps, line passes, and even cash rebates. In fact, if you play your "reels" right, you can virtually enjoy free vacations doing just what you like to do best in the casinos — playing the slots! And that's not bad at all.

Why all the fuss?

Given the large amount of profits casinos earn from their slots players, and their recognition of the importance of the revenue they generate, you, as a slots player today, are king, baby. No longer are the table games the real bread and butter of a casino. This is not the 70s anymore. It's the new era of the slot machines; they comprise more than 50% of a typical casino's action!

Casinos rely more and more on their slots players to generate bottom line profits and have steadily increased the space allocated to slots to reflect this. Now, anywhere you go in a modern casino, you see them, you hear them, you *feel* them. The slot machines are expanding throughout casinos like some blob out of a 60s era flick. As fast as their presence expands, new players expand with them, plopping the coins into the bellies of the one armed beasts.

Slots players are no longer taken for granted. With slots revenues in the billions worldwide, casinos are realizing who their important players really are and are actively pursuing their patronage. Comps, incentives, and bonuses, once reserved for table players, are now in the full domain of the slots player.

That's great news for slots players because casinos are motivated to get you to their machines as opposed to their competitors' machines, a situation I'll show you how to take advantage of for your full benefit.

About the Slots Clubs

Slots clubs are basically enrollment programs that players sign up for as members. There is no charge to become a member, but lots of benefits. The concept is simple. Once enrolled as a member, the casinos will issue a member card with the player's name and card number. These cards are inserted into the machines prior to play and automatically track the player's betting action. The more action a player gives the casino, the greater the benefits he enjoys just for playing the machines. And what could be better?

For example, in some casinos, players can accrue enough credits after approximately just one hour of action at the $1 machines, or 2-3 hours at the 25¢ machines, that they can qualify for benefits. Benefits and comps are all a function of the amount of money played. And that, in casino parlance is called *action*. Action, to a casino is not some theoretical concept. It's the total amount of money played. For example if you're playing $1 slots, three coins at a time, and play 500 spins, you've given the casino $1,500 worth of action, 500 spins by $3 each. If you're playing quarters, five at a time to a machine, and play 1,000 spins, your action is equal to 5,000 quarters, or $1,250.

Note that the action given to a machine or a casino is not measured by how much you've won or lost, but the total amount of plays multiplied by the amount bet. Thus, using othe above example at the $1 machines, whether you've won $115 overall, or lost $115, to the casino, your action is still that same $1,500. Plenty good to start earning comps, and really good if you've got a $115 profit to show as well.

And that's why slots clubs are so great. If you're going to be playing the machines anyway, you're guaranteed "winnings," so to speak, by dint of the simple fact that your action is earning rewards. For example, if you're playing the 25 cent slots for several hours, and drop $23 at the machines, but earn two free $15 dinner comps, you're not feeling so bad. You've come out ahead of the game.

These slots cards are great tracking devices that not only record a player's total action and the total amount of money wagered at the machine, but keep track of a player's behavior so that the casinos can better understand their customers: the machines they like to play, in what denominations, and how long each machine is played.

Each casino has their own slots program, some with greater benefits than others. But all are worth joining if you plan to play slots at a casino, and especially if you plan on playing a lot of slots.

Slots clubs began as an experiment at the Sands Casino in Atlantic City in 1982 as a method to attract and keep slots players in their casino. In 1984, the Golden Nugget introduced this concept to Las Vegas, and as they say, the rest is history. Almost every casino today in Las Vegas or Atlantic City has an actively promoted slots club. The few that don't are at a tremendous marketing disadvantage. After all, why would a serious slots player patronize a casino offering nothing special to attract his or her play when the casino next door has a great slots club with tons of inducements? The answer is simple, they wouldn't.

While the casinos are eager to induce players into their casinos with attractive slots club benefits, the players are just as eager to reap the rewards for doing what they were going to do anyway - play the slots. The trick is learning how to play the system for the full amount of the awards.

Should You Join a Slots Club?

Absolutely! If you're going to be playing the slots, you should definitely join. You have nothing to lose and everything to gain. The application requires nothing more than your basic information; the membership has nothing to do with income level or credit information. Outside of the few minutes it might take to apply, there is no other effort needed to enjoy the many benefits.

Some players feel that they don't gamble enough to even bother signing up. *Au contraire*. It's not how much you're willing to risk at the tables, it's the amount of action you give those machines that counts. Well, you might say, I'm only going to play with $20. That $20 may earn you $50, $100, or more in comps if your luck is good.

Let's say you get on a roll with that $20 and work it for several hours or more before walking away with $22, for $2 in profit. Or, let's just say that the machine swallowed up that $20. Either way, you've possibly generated enough action to receive some comps. In total, if you add up all the bets you made during that playing session, it will may add up to hundreds of dollars in action. That's a lot more significant than the mere $20 you thought you were wagering. *The actual action was much higher than the actual wager.*

Many players don't realize this and lose out on benefits they otherwise could have accumulated.

Getting Started

Joining a slots club is as easy as filling out an application form. The Slots Hosts are usually located in the rear of the casinos, but if you can't find them, ask any of the personnel and they will send you in the right direction. I find that the security guards are the best to ask, especially in the casinos that have a security officer posted at a central desk near the cashier's cage.

The application process for joining is simple and the application itself won't take long to fill out. The casinos are mostly concerned that they can properly identify you and that they can get you on their mailing list to keep you abreast of the latest and most exciting developments from their slots club.

Keep in mind that this application is simply a formality — nobody is going to get turned down. They have no interest in your credit history or how much money you make. This is not a credit application, only an application to get you going to initiate membership.

Choosing the Best Slots Clubs

In the beginning, getting the most for your gambling buck is a matter of researching the various casinos you're interested in and finding out who has the most generous incentives. Many casinos will give you a printed schedule showing how the rewards work.

Comparing the different programs for their benefits is the best way to decide what's right for you. But this is the information, the leg work, so to speak, you'll need to do as you're getting established among the various clubs.

Others won't give you any information at all, and in fact, will claim they don't know the structure of their point system. These casinos should be avoided.

The real way to get going with the slots clubs and reap the maximum benefits is to join them all, or at least as many as is practical! This doesn't mean you have to play in all of them. You should focus your playing in the clubs with the best machines and the best rewards. The others can lie dormant until the time is right. Meanwhile, you'll be on all these clubs' mailing lists, and when there is a great slots promotion, you'll be the first to know. Hey, these casinos know that they have a lot of competition and they want to get you in their door. That means they need to give you huge incentives for you to make your next trip to their casino.

With offers galore coming in, you can start cherry-picking the best deals. Then you're on your way to all the freebies Las Vegas has to offer. With some good timing, and a little luck, you may even find yourself with a free vacation - rooms, meals, shows, cash rebates, and even *more* points built up for *more* comps.

Getting Started on the Comps

As soon as you sign up for a slots club, the casino may issue you freebies and incentives as your sign-up bonus. This could include meal or show discounts or comps, tee shirts, bonus plays — really anything at all the casino is using as a promotion to get you to sign up for their club. These incentives frequently change depending on the promotions people.

The first thing that happens when you sign up for a slots club is that you are issued a card. This card identifies you as a player and a member of the slots club that issued it, and will be used to track your play at the machines. The casinos will have you on file and in the system. Armed with this card, you'll earn rewards credits every time you play.

Step one to insuring at least some promotional offers is to put that card to use right away with a little action in the casino. This lets them know that they have a "live" player, and will make them work that much harder to pile you with incentives.

Even if you don't use your card right away in a casino's machines, they will have you down on their mailing list, and will still entice you with offers through the mail. The idea here, as with any mailing list, is that you're an interested player. With the right offer and the right timing, they may get you back into the casinos and playing. If you're planning a trip to Vegas and a casino sends you some comp food tickets to get you in the door, that strategy just might work, to everyone's benefit.

Some slots clubs may want to qualify their players, that is, make sure you're really a *player*, one who is going to give them action and has proven so by already playing — not just someone who shows up on any list that he can get on. Or, perhaps casinos may give the qualified player better offers. In any case, slots clubs change their offers all the time, depending upon their marketing programs, but I find that giving the card at least a little play is the safest way to go to get the ball rolling.

The next step toward really qualifying you as a *player* is to meet the casino's minimum level of play toward their first qualifying level of play. Again, the minimum playing requirements vary from casino to casino, and can vary from one month to another as policies and the competitive environment changes. You'll have to see where things stand if you've been away from the casinos for a while, and see if what was a good program last time is still good, or if perhaps, you find a slots club you like even better for this trip.

Casinos that really value you as a customer will let you know up front what they expect from you. It will be spelled out in black and white just how much action you need to generate for the awards programs to kick in. Some casinos publish newsletters, which will give you the ins and outs of the promotional details. Some might provide that information verbally, while the less inspired casinos will keep it a dark secret, and of course generate less action from players who don't know what they can expect from their patronage.

Typically, and again this varies completely from one program to another, approximately one hour worth of action at the $1 slots, or 2-3 hours at the 25¢ machines will kick in the first tier of bonuses and comps. Faster players may reach these levels a little faster, slower players may take a little longer. The critical element the casinos are looking for is the amount of action, how much money is wagered into the machines, not how long you happen to be sitting in front of a machine warming a chair.

The casinos want *action*. You give it to them, and they'll kick back in with their incentives.

How the Slots Card Works

The most important factor in earning your full playing credits at the slot machines is to use your slots card. Every slot machine in the casino has a card reader that will accept your club card for play. These are typically found in the front of the machines, though they may be on the sides. The new IGT series of machines, the most prevalent machines on the market, contain their readers right in front, in easy view of the player.

If for some reason you can't find the reader, have trouble inserting your card into it, or have any other problem, call over one of the slots personnel. They'll be glad to help you get set up. That is what they are there for.

Your first move, upon approaching a machine and readying yourself for play, is to insert your card into the card reader. Upon insertion, the card will usually identify you by name, though sometimes the casino will have a theme greeting instead.

What if You Lose Your Card

If you've left your card back home or in your casino room, or have even lost it altogether, no problem. Go to the slots host and they'll give you a replacement card upon presentation of your ID. This happens all the time to players. Casinos will be happy to set you up again with your card and get you back to the machines.

Earning the First Level of Slots Club Benefits

Once you know the minimal levels of play you need to meet to qualify for the programs' first level of benefits, the only variable that affect the time it takes to get to that first benefit level are the speed of play (how many spins on average you play per hour) and the average number of coins you play per spin. Or to put both those variables together, in essence, the formula boils down to how many coins you play per hour. The more coins per hour you play, the faster you accumulate the action required by a casino to reach activation levels.

How do the casinos determine this first level? First you must understand how casinos rate a player's slots action in general, and then how they reward that action.

Casinos generally rate a player's action on a point system, awarding a certain number of points for each level of dollars played. You may receive one point per dollar played, one point per $20 played, or even ten points per $1 played. But none of this means anything unless you know what these points mean. Each point earned is relative to the value given to it by that particular casino.

Tip for Earning Extra Points

You can earn action points at more than just slot machines. Your slots card is also good for racking up points at the video poker machines and often at all the other machines in the casino. There are even casinos that will give you credits at the table games.

Each casino has their own point system and activation levels, and it is only by knowing these levels that you can make sense of which slots program is good, and which one is not quite as attractive. For example, getting ten points for $1 won't mean anything if the activation level for this casino requires you to spend twice as much time playing your preferred denomination machine as another casino. In other words, 1,000 points at one casino may be of more value to you than 1,000 points at a different one, and may even be of more value than 10,000 points at another casino that throws points around like Italian lira.

There are other ways that casinos rate a player's action at their slots, such as time played, but typically speaking, casinos will use the total dollar value action wagered by the player. The total number of coins placed into the machines multiplied by their dollar value is the most accurate and fair measure of play anyway. Playing three dollars a spin and spinning the reels 300 times yields an exact amount of action — $900. Another player may spend just as much time at that machine, but put in only one third as much play. Obviously, the first player is more valuable to the casino, and is a player the casinos want to encourage even more than the second.

Casinos don't want to reward players just for time spent at a machine, who perhaps just sit there soaking in the free drinks and the atmosphere, and accruing points with little play. Casinos want action, and there is no better measure of that action than adding up the coins played and the reels spun.

Point Expiration

Your points can expire if you haven't returned to a casino within twelve months of your last visit. You'll have to ask your slots host if this applies to you. If so, make sure to redeem any awards before expiration.

On the following pages, I've put together five Action Charts that show the amount of time you have to play at different denomination machines to accrue different amounts of play at a casino.

Action Chart - $1,000

Coin	Coins Played	Speed of Play	
		Fast	**Slow**
5¢	5	10 hours	11 hours
	3	16 hours	18 hours
	1	50 hours	60 hours
25¢	5	2 hours	2.5 hours
	3	3.5 hours	4 hours
	1	10 hours	12 hours
$1	5	30 minutes	45 minutes
	3	45 minutes	1 hour
	1	2.5 hours	3 hours
$5	5	6 minutes	7 minutes
	3	9 minutes	11 minutes
	1	30 minutes	37 minutes

This chart shows approximately how long it would take to reach **$1,000** in action. It does not takes into account the house payback (return percentage) since it is only tracking the number of bets multiplied by the size of the bet. Keep in mind that this chart is only an approximation, and that every individual's speed is different.

You see by the chart, that the fewer coins played per pull, the longer it takes to reach the level shown. Similarly, the slower the player's average playing speed, the longer it will take.

Since the average player will play the full amount of coins allowed by the machine, and the experienced player tends to go at faster paces, you can expect that the action levels will be hit more often at the faster pace.

Action Chart - $2,000

| | | Speed of Play | |
Coin	Coins Played	Fast	Slow
5¢	5	20 hours	22.5 hours
	3	32.5 hours	37.5 hours
	1	100 hours	120 hours
25¢	5	4 hours	4.5 hours
	3	6.5 hours	7.5 hours
	1	20 hours	24 hours
$1	5	1 hour	1.5 hours
	3	1.5 hours	2 hours
	1	5 hours	6 hours
$5	5	12 minutes	14 minutes
	3	19 minutes	22 minutes
	1	1 hour	1.25 hours

This chart shows approximately how long it would take to reach **$2,000** in action. It does not take into account the house payback (return percentage) since it is only tracking the number of bets multiplied by the size of the bet. Keep in mind that this chart is only an approximation, and that every individual's speed is different.

You see by the chart that the fewer coins played per pull, the longer it takes to reach the level shown. Similarly, the slower the player's average playing speed, the longer it will take.

Since the average player will play the full amount of coins allowed by the machine, and the experienced player tends to go at faster paces, you can expect that the action levels will be hit more often at the faster pace.

Action Chart - $3,000

Coin	Coins Played	Speed of Play	
		Fast	**Slow**
5¢	5	30 hours	34 hours
	3	48 hours	57 hours
	1	150 hours	180 hours
25¢	5	6 hours	7 hours
	3	9 hours	11.5 hours
	1	30 hours	36 hours
$1	5	1.5 hour	2.25 hours
	3	2.25 hours	3 hours
	1	7.5 hours	9 hours
$5	5	18 minutes	21 minutes
	3	28 minutes	33 minutes
	1	1.5 hours	2 hours

This chart shows approximately how long it would take to reach **$3,000** in action. It does not take into account the house payback (return percentage) since it is only tracking the number of bets multiplied by the size of the bet. Keep in mind that this chart is only an approximation, and that every individual's speed is different.

You see by the chart that the fewer coins played per pull, the longer it takes to reach the level shown. Similarly, the slower the player's average playing speed, the longer it will take.

Since the average player will play the full amount of coins allowed by the machine, and the experienced player tends to go at faster paces, you can expect that the action levels will be hit more often at the faster pace.

Action Chart - $4,000

Coin	Coins Played	Speed of Play	
		Fast	Slow
5¢	5	40 hours	45 hours
	3	65 hours	75 hours
	1	200 hours	240 hours
25¢	5	8 hours	9 hours
	3	13 hours	15 hours
	1	40 hours	48 hours
$1	5	2 hours	3 hours
	3	3 hours	4 hours
	1	10 hours	12 hours
$5	5	24 minutes	28 minutes
	3	38 minutes	44 minutes
	1	2 hours	2.5 hours

This chart shows approximately how long it would take to reach **$4,000** in action. It does not take into account the house payback (return percentage) since it is only tracking the number of bets multiplied by the size of the bet. Keep in mind that this chart is only an approximation, and that every individual's speed is different.

You see by the chart that the fewer coins played per pull, the longer it takes to reach the level shown. Similarly, the slower the player's average playing speed, the longer it will take.

Since the average player will play the full amount of coins allowed by the machine, and the experienced player tends to go at faster paces, you can expect that the action levels will be hit more often at the faster pace.

Action Chart - $5,000

Coin	Coins Played	Speed of Play	
		Fast	**Slow**
5¢	5	50 hours	56 hours
	3	81 hours	94 hours
	1	250 hours	300 hours
25¢	5	10 hours	11.5 hours
	3	16.5 hours	19 hours
	1	50 hours	60 hours
$1	5	2.5 hour	4 hours
	3	4 hours	5 hours
	1	12.5 hours	15 hours
$5	5	30 minutes	35 minutes
	3	46 minutes	55 minutes
	1	2.5 hours	3 hours

This chart shows approximately how long it would take to reach **$5,000** in action. It does not take into account the house payback (return percentage) since it is only tracking the number of bets multiplied by the size of the bet. Keep in mind that this chart is only an approximation, and that every individual's speed is different.

You see by the chart that the fewer coins played per pull, the longer it takes to reach the level shown. Similarly, the slower the player's average playing speed, the longer it will take.

Since the average player will play the full amount of coins allowed by the machine, and the experienced player tends to go at faster paces, you can expect that the action levels will be hit more often at the faster pace.

Action Chart - $10,000

Coin	Coins Played	Speed of Play	
		Fast	Slow
5¢	5	100 hours	115 hours
	3	165 hours	190 hours
	1	500 hours	600 hours
25¢	5	20 hours	23 hours
	3	33 hours	38 hours
	1	100 hours	120 hours
$1	5	5 hours	7.5 hours
	3	7.5 hours	10 hours
	1	25 hours	30 hours
$5	5	1 hour	1.25 hours
	3	1.5 hours	2 hours
	1	5 hours	6.25 hours

This chart shows approximately how long it would take to reach **$10,000** in action. It does not take into account the house payback (return percentage) since it is only tracking the number of bets multiplied by the size of the bet. Keep in mind that this chart is only an approximation, and that every individual's speed is different.

You see by the chart that the fewer coins played per pull, the longer it takes to reach the level shown. Similarly, the slower the player's average playing speed, the longer it will take.

Since the average player will play the full amount of coins allowed by the machine, and the experienced player tends to go at faster paces, you can expect that the action levels will be hit more often at the faster pace.

Planning Ahead

So, remember to prepare for your next trip to Las Vegas, or wherever you might be gambling, by contacting the slots clubs at the casinos where you might be playing, in order to get yourself setup in advance. Most casinos have toll free 800 numbers, and would be glad to give you the information.

Of course, you can always sign up when you arrive, and that's no problem, but by alerting the casino that you're coming, or might be coming, they might send you incentives and comp tickets to make sure they get you to visit and play.

20 Winning Strategies at Slots

Players are always asking me, "how can there be winning strategies at slots? All you do is pull the handle and either win or lose, isn't that right?" The answer, is that it isn't right. There *are* better ways to play and we'll go over them in this chapter.

There are ways to maximize your chances of winning in the short term by playing the proper amount of coins, strategies to increase your chances of the big jackpot, strategies to take advantage of the benefits casinos give to slots players, better casinos to play in and better machines to choose from, and finally, ways to maximize wins and minimize losses through money management strategies. Knowing how to properly play the slots can make the difference between winning and losing, and this chapter will show you those tips and secrets.

Surprisingly, there are lots of strategies you can pursue for such a simple game. By following my advice, you'll do much better than the average player, and at times, under the right conditions, you may actually find yourself with an edge.

Let's get to it. Following is the first of my twenty winning strategy tips.

WINNING STRATEGY #1

Jurisdictions for Better Odds – Choose Better Casinos

Yes it is true: Las Vegas casinos, on average, give small and medium coin players ($1 and less) a much better shake at the machines than their Atlantic City counterparts. Large coin players ($5 and up), have a similar game in either locale, based on the last figures I've seen. I have examined reports published by both the Nevada State Gaming Control Board and the New Jersey Casino Control Commission, and saw significant differences in payback percentages.

So for this winning slots tip, if you have a choice and are a small or medium coin player, play Las Vegas slots over Atlantic City slots.

How about the rest of you slots players taking on the slots in the riverboat states, Indian reservations and various other locations that contain slot machines? While it would be beyond the scope of this book to publish a complete guide to average paybacks nationwide or worldwide (and often, these figures are not available), the general rule is that the more competition in an area, the better the odds.

Since you generally have little choice in choosing areas to play — basically where you happen to be is where you'll play — use the other winning tips presented in this section for maximizing your odds at the slots. It does you no good to know that the odds may be better in Las Vegas when you are playing slots in Louisiana or Illinois — just as it does a New Yorker no good to know that movies may cost $7 in Idaho and $10 in the Big Apple.

Below is a chart showing the average payout percentages by coin amount in Nevada casinos, as published by the Nevada Gaming Control Board, for the one year period ending in September 1996.

Payback Percentage by Coin - Las Vegas

Coin	Payback
5¢	92%
10$	92.5%
25¢	95%
50¢	95.5%
$1	95.5%
$5	96.5%
$25	97%

All figures are rounded out to the nearest 1/2 percent.

Note, I don't have figures on the $100 and $500 slots, but it is a safe presumption that they are at least as loose as the $25 machines, most likely a little better.

You see that the larger the denomination of coins played in Las Vegas, the greater the average payback percentage given by the casino. This is no coincidence. Casinos would like to encourage players to play at the higher coin levels and encourage them to do so by paying out more for the larger coins. While this is not posted anywhere in the casino, nor is it common knowledge, players know when they're having success at a machine and when they're not. Higher percentage payouts do get noticed, and with player win satisfaction at a reasonable level, the coins keep flowing and the player will keep playing.

The idea of paying higher percentages to big coin players mirrors the thinking as to the placement of machines. More frequent winners means players stay encouraged to play the higher levels and the machines gets more action. Translation: more profits. While casinos make less percentage-wise from the higher coin machines, they more than make up for it in action and overall profits.

In Atlantic City, the payback percentages for lower denomination machines ($1 or less), are significantly lower than in the more competitive Las Vegas casino environment, with average paybacks 3%-6% less. On the $5, $25, and larger machines, the paybacks are competitive with Las Vegas big coin machines.

In Atlantic City, you'll never play a machine that pays out less than 83%. The New Jersey Casino Control Commission requires that slot machines in Atlantic City payback at least that amount on all slot machines.

While Las Vegas machines generally pay much better, it is interesting to note that the Nevada State Gaming Control Board sets no minimums on slot payback percentages. And if you play off the beaten path in areas not good for slots players, as we discussed earlier, these machines will suck up every rock you stick into them.

WINNING STRATEGY #2

Find Casinos with Better Paying Machines

Your first rule as a player is to keep to casinos that cater to serious slots players as a primary source of income. If a casino is looking to attract serious slots business, it has got to give these people something to whoop about so that it can keep them as steady players. In the old days, this meant having machines with a good payback. Nowadays, it also means having an aggressive slots club rich with rewards for their good players.

So how do you get a sense of when a casino is good for slots players? Check it out. If the casino is buzzing with slots players, that's a good sign. It's not the end in itself, but it is a good sign that it is good for slots players. It's similar to scoping out a restaurant in an unfamiliar area. Lots of patrons are a good sign. An empty atmosphere doesn't bode well. Thus, go where the action is.

WINNING STRATEGY #3

Avoid Locales with Sucker Machines

I already talked about looking for places that had lots of players, so obviously the converse is true: avoid places where there are few players and gravitate toward places where you feel excitement in the slots area.

But there's another principle that is very true as well: do not play slots in places where the slots business is incidental to the main business. Why? Because the customers that play the machines in these establishments are not there to play these machines. The are there to do something else. They see the machines, play them a little, and then move on. These types of slots places can get away with horrific odds because the players aren't likely to hang around anyway, so why not take the most that could be taken?

The thinking here is that the player will drop coins into the machines gratuitously. And that in fact is what happens at these venues. What kinds of places are these? If you want to get good odds, avoid playing slot machines in the following places: Airports, Laundromats, Bars, Grocery and Convenience stores, Gas stations, and the like. These are places where slot machines will swallow your money as fast as you can feed them.

Locations within a casino are often important as well. That slot machine in the bathroom can be counted on to have the worst payback in the entire casino.

Think about it: Who is going to be hanging around a bathroom very long for the purpose of gambling? (If you can think of someone that might, well, let the lord have mercy.) Slots lining a restaurant or buffet line will probably be set with lower percentages, since the average player will have just seconds or minutes of playing time before his or her spot moves on closer to the gluttony that awaits in the dining area.

Serious players are going to park themselves in front of machines for hours on end, and will only do so if enough positive reinforcement is had from winning pulls at the machines. Stick them in front of enough lemons in a casino, and that casino won't be seeing them again.

WINNING STRATEGY #4

Choose Your Spots in Local Casinos

You already know that payout percentages vary from machine to machine within a casino. Within a particular bank of machines, at first glance, there's not much to see. If visiting a local casino (a casino off the beaten path that is heavily frequented by locals) see what the experienced players do.

If, for example, they stay away from a particular bank of machines, my advice is that you do too. They know something from experience that you'll learn quickly if you sit down at that ghost bank: These machines don't cough up too many winners. Play the machines they play, and avoid the machines they avoid.

WINNING STRATEGY #5

Playing the Proper Coin

Depending upon the machine, you have a choice of playing anywhere from one to five coins at a time on a typical machine. Some machines may take two coins maximum, some may allow you to place five at a time. These are the typical machines you'll find on the floors now.

A very important principle to keep in mind at most slot machines, that is, the ones that pay proportionately more for all coins played on the big jackpot, is to play the maximum number of coins allowed on each play. You'll need to see the payout schedule for the machine you're playing to see if this applies, but most likely it will.

Like the video poker machines where the progressive jackpot or full coin payout on a royal flush is maximized only when all five coins are played, the big jackpot payouts in slots only earn out to their full potential when all coins are played.

For example, the jackpot on one coin played may be 1,000 coins, while that for two on a machine may be 3,000 coins, not the 2,000 coins you might expect if it was proportional. Obviously, on a machine with a disproportionate payoff for more coins, you want to take advantage of it. If this means you're playing for more than you would like to, then you need to switch to a lower denomination machine.

This principle holds true on all progressives. On these slots, the full number of coins must be played to win the big jackpot. That is standard. Any lesser number of coins will negate the big jackpot and give you only a minor win at the machine, that is, minor compared to the riches you could have had.

For example, on a *Cool Millions* machines that I saw, the difference between playing two coins and three coins, the machine maximum, would give you ulcers had you not played correctly and hit the two coin payout, which was 25,000 coins on the quarter machine, $6,250. The three coin payout was $615,000 at the time! That is a major difference.

The same holds true for many of the other progressives. If you're playing at a machine with big jackpot potential, you're paying a price in smaller returns as you go for the big win. (We'll talk more about that later.) It only makes sense to play these machines the right way — with the full number of coins that the machine requires for you to qualify for the progressive. You'll only achieve the maximum potential on a progressive this way.

If you don't like playing the full number of coins allowed, you shouldn't be playing the progressives. That's a very important rule to keep in mind.

On non-progressive machines, there is often a payout difference as well on the bigger money payout. For example, one coin might pay 800, two coins 1600, and three coins, 4,000. That's a big difference. If you're uncomfortable playing at that denomination because of the full number of coins, you may be able to find smaller denomination machines that allow your bankroll to handle the full coin allowance.

If you're playing buy-your-pay machines, you absolutely must play the full number of coins to get the benefits of not only the big jackpot payout, but also the lesser ones, which may be void if you didn't put enough coins in.

WINNING STRATEGY #6

Playing the Best Coin for Your Bankroll

As a player, you have a choice of a large variety of machines, from the 5¢ slots, which somehow, still hold space on the casino floors today, to the 10¢, 25¢, 50¢, $1.00, $5.00, $25.00 and even higher coin machines.

While, as I determined earlier, the larger denomination slots tend to average a higher rate of return, that is not a factor in choosing a machine. It should not even enter into the equation. Sure, we always want to go for the highest percentage possible, but using larger bets than we normally might handle is a formula for disaster and nothing good will come of it.

The most important factor before ever approaching any machine, gaming table, or any type of gamble, is always to determine the amount you're not only willing to gamble. You should never, under any circumstances, gamble with money you cannot afford to lose either financially or emotionally. That is a rule that can never be broken.

So before you ask yourself the question, "what is the best denomination machine to play?" first ask yourself how much you are willing to put up, as your playing stake will determine the proper type of machine you should play. Be sure to read the money management chapter carefully where I talk about this issue in-depth.

Though it is true that, as an industry average, the higher the denomination coin played, the greater the winning percentage returned by the casinos — do not get waylaid by this information. As I've stated earlier, every machine has its own dynamic. An IGT 25¢ Double Diamond machine may pay 91% while the exact type 25¢ Double Diamond next to it on the bank may give out 96%. A 5¢ machine across the way may pay back 97%, while the one next to it may give back only 88%.

According to the strategies I've laid out in this book, each machine must be viewed on a case by case basis so that the best and most optimal strategy might be followed.

While the general winning formula follows the guideline of always playing the games and making the bets which afford you the best odds, there is always one overriding factor that comes first in thinking as a winning player: money management.

The first playing decision is to decide the proper amount you're willing to wager. Never play at a level of risk or affordability that is over your head, and that goes for all stages of gambling. Play in the games and the arenas that are at your level and you will never get hurt. Play over your head, and you just might get hurt for a lot more than you can handle.

You never want to put too many eggs in one basket, no matter how good the odds are. The plain facts are that anything can happen. And that's considering an example where the odds favor you. That's not the case in slots. The odds are in the house's favor, sometimes heavily so, especially for the unsophisticated player.

You certainly don't want to bet over your head, especially not for an extra percent or two. Face it, it's much better to play x amount at a 95% payback (5% house edge) than four times x amount at a 96% payback (4% edge). While you lose less percentage-wise at the larger bet, you lose almost four times as much overall for the same amount of playing time. That never makes sense.

Don't lose sight of your overall goal in playing slots. It's to relax and have a good time. That can only be done while playing within your means and at a stake you're comfortable with. If the best percentage you can get at a slot machine is 95% and you want to play, that's fine. If you can grab 97% or even 99%, so much the better. Keep to these basics — the basics of having fun and entertaining yourself — and you can't go wrong. Think about all that while eating your comped buffet and watching the comped show.

WINNING STRATEGY #7

Bump Up to Single Coin Play

Here's an inside tip for improving your odds at the machines. I spoke earlier about playing the maximum number of coins to get the best odds, and how larger denomination machines average a higher payback percentage. Sometimes you'll find machines you like at a one-step higher denomination which doesn't penalize you for playing the full number of coins. For example, you may find a machine which gives you no more proportionately for the first coin played, than for the third or fifth coin.

All things being equal, if you like the same machine at a higher denomination than you usually play follow this strategy: Bump up! For example, if you're a quarter player (investing three or five quarters per pull — 75¢ or $1.25), bump up to the $1 machine at *single coin play*. Similarly, a 5¢ player can move up to the 25¢ machines, and a $1 player can bump up to the $5 machines.

This is a great way to take advantage of the higher percentages being paid on the larger denomination machines. Remember, this strategy is only good when there is no penalty for single coin play.

One other caution that is very, very important: *Never* double bump denominations. That is, don't go from 5¢ to $1, or 25¢ to $5 machines. Money management is of utmost importance in the winning formula, and betting over your bankroll, which a double bump will do, is the worst thing you can do.

The single bump with a single coin play is the maximum correct play.

WINNING STRATEGY #8

Escape from Cold Machines

You'll sometimes find machines that are so cold that you can't seem to win anything. This machine is probably set low and you're feeling the pain. If it's obviously not paying off for you, it's obvious that you need to change machines.

Besides the low payout of the machine, there is another reason to leave: You're most likely not enjoying yourself and are thinking that you should leave this machine and try another. *Follow your instincts*. Players always have a lousy feeling after dropping endless amounts of money into a machine that started bad and gave them bad feelings.

First rule: If you're not comfortable with a particular machine, go to one where you *are* comfortable. After all, why play machines that give you bad feelings? Stick to the slots that give you a positive feeling; that's where you'll get your maximum enjoyment.

By the same token, avoid playing machines that are "ripe" for winnings. Being ripe for a jackpot means someone, yourself or another player, has been pouring coins in to some one-armed hog to little avail. As I said above, if it ain't paying, you shouldn't be playing.

WINNING STRATEGY #9

Stick with Hot Machines

When a machine is hot and paying off for you like crazy, stick with it like glue. When you have a good one, play if for all it's worth. A hot machine generally means you found a machine with a high payback return, a loose one.

As long as you keep winning, it would be a major mistake to change to an unproven machine. However, should the tide start to turn, and money starts being sucked back into the machine, use smart money management principles and leave the machine a winner. That's always a smart way to play.

Similarly, if your machine is paying so-so, and you see another player leave a machine that's been hot, grab that machine while it's still available. You always want to play the machine that appears to be the best payer because it usually *is* the best payer.

IMPORTANT POINT
Understanding Hot and Cold Advice

Don't take my advice on playing hot machines and avoiding cold ones to mean that I think slot machine spins are on a memory basis concerning winners and losers — because they're not.

Machines are not due for anything, not for a win, not for a loss, not for spinning over and doing cartwheels. Each spin of the reel is independently generated and has as much to do with the next spin as it did with the last spin - that is, nothing. They're random, or are at least as close to random as the manufacturers can make them, which is very close to truly random. There are probabilities of reels lining up in a certain way and you are paid on those probabilities when the combinations are winners.

When I talk about hot and cold machines, I only speak of using recent history of the machines to understand that there may be a pattern of better or worse payouts, a pattern that is totally tied in to the probabilities of how the machine was set. While a small sampling is really not sufficient for a true empirical determination, it's all the information we have, and often, it will be all we need.

Don't Ever Leave a Winning Machine

Unless you really had enough play for a day, or need to go elsewhere, don't ever leave a winning machine. When you got a hot one, ride it for all it's worth. But once it stops paying good, back off, and *then* take a break - with all your profits.

WINNING STRATEGY #10

Mega-Progressive Strategy

There is one aspect concerning frequency of wins that you need to understand to increase your winning chances. Not all 95% payback machines give you an equal chance of winning, nor do all 90% payback machines. Huh? Doesn't 95% and 95%, and 90% and 90% equal one another?

Yes and no. It depends how the cut has been arrived at to get those figures.

When all is said and done, that is, over the long run, two 95% machines will pay out equally and your chances of winning are equal. But the long run with these mega-progressives are gauged by millions and millions of pulls, so many pulls that just a handful of players of the many million playing get that monster prize. The rest, eaten up by that longshot prize, suffer with fewer and shorter wins.

I'll explain this concept using three theoretical slots machine as an example.

We'll say that we have ten million dollars in bets, with a pool of nine million dollars in prizes. That makes these slots 90% payback machines. One hundred thousand players are playing the game, and on average, bet 100 pulls at $1 each, for a total bet of $100 per player. $100 multiplied by 100,000 players equals ten million pulls on the handle, at $1 each.

On all these machines, we'll assume that the law of averages perfectly plays itself out on these ten million pulls, so that the end result sees players taking back nine million in prizes out of the ten million bet, for an average loss of 10%, or $10 per player out of the $100 they bet. The casino will win that 10% and show a one million dollar profit on these machines. That will be their hold.

What will be interesting is that the following three 90% payback machines will yield the same total for the casino no matter how the cake is cut. The difference is simply how the pie is divided. (From cakes to pies, you can see that I'm getting nearer to the comp buffet.)

Let's now look at the three different machines to see how it affects a player's chances: the *Mega-Machine*, the *Roll' Em Winner*, and the *Small Potato*. Note that the *Mega-Machine* and *Small Potato* machines are not based on actual machines, but are used as extremes to illustrate the importance of a payback schedule. The *Roll'em Winner* approximates actual machines you'll find today.

Machine One: Mega-Machine

The Mega-Machine offers the winning player an eight million dollar jackpot when it is hit. This player will be set for life and will be one very happy camper. The eight million dollars paid out over 20 years comes out to a $400,000 per year check (less the IRS cut), or for the working man or woman who could live without their 9-5 job, instant retirement and a dream come true. That hope, and all the stories of other big winners, keeps this type of machine hopping.

For one player, this is a dream come true. for the other 999,999 players, it leaves a slim pool of money to win, and consequently, big losses.

The other one million dollars in the pool will be split up in winnings, on average, by all 100,000 players. (The big jackpot winner is also hitting little winners as well.) One million dollars split up among 100,000 players comes out to an average return of $10 each. This means that on this machine, the average player will win back only $10 of the $100 played. Ouch! That's only a 10% average payback for all the other chumps, all 99,999 of them! Losing $90 out of every $100 is highway robbery.

Some players will do better and some will do even worse than the 10% With such a small pool of other players winning money, very few winners emerge. It is really just one big unhappy pool of losers. Compare this to the 90% payback you thought you would see.

Obviously this is not a very attractive machine. Note that this example is an extreme and no big jackpot slot would, in proportion, return so much to one player and so little to the rest. If they did, no one would want to play. It would be too much of a sucker pull and players would learn that quite quickly.

Machine Two: Roll 'em Winner

This machine is a lot more sane and gets a lot more action. It will average fifty $10,000 winners, and spread out the remainder of the $8,500,000 in winning pulls over an assortment of different combinations. Where winning pulls on the *Mega-Machine* were few and far between, the *Roll 'em Winner* is chugging out payouts left and right.

While the *Roll 'em Winner* machine doesn't put any one on easy street, it also doesn't restrict itself to just one Lucky Louie. Now we have 50 eager beavers that bagged $10,000 in winnings on just one pull (plus whatever they accumulated on the other pulls), which adds up to a lot more people returning from their trips with stories of the big hit. And for the casino's benefit, fifty very happy players are telling everyone they know about how much fun they had and getting all their friends and family psyched for their own trips to the casinos.

The other $8,500,000 in payouts is spread out, on average, among the full assortment of 100,000 players (including the 50 big winners), to the tune of $85 per player. That averages out to an 85% return on the $100 bet. Again, some will win more on average and some will win less. But there will be a lot of winners after the 100 pulls. Most players here will see some winning action and will have enjoyed themselves much more than the *Mega-Machine* players who pulled the handle in about as barren a winning desert as you can find.

Machine Three: Small Potatoes

This fictional slots is designed as a machine to give constant reinforcement to its players by enticing them with lots of small wins. On average, out of every ten pulls, on average, six will pay back winners. The wins are small and little to get excited about, but they're wins nonetheless. One out of ten wins will pay three coins per coin played, one will pay two coins per coin played, and four will pay one coin per coin played. Thus, nine coins will be returned for every 10 played.

This may not be incredibly exciting, but there is a lot of little action. Since there are no big wins getting pulled out of the overall payout pool, the average player will split the nine million dollar pool equally, and each player will average a 90% payback, or $90 returned on every $100 they bet. In short, there will be a lot of winners

Comparing the Three Machines

The three machines we've shown, the *Roll 'em Winner*, the *Mega-Machine*, and the *Small Potatoes*, all share one thing. When all is said and done, the players win back nine million dollars of the ten million they bet. And the casino win their 10%. All the machines I talked about here were 90% machines.

Where these machines were not equal is in how the winning pool is split. The machines on the two extremes, are extremes that are not realistic to today's market and wouldn't be successful or inviting to the players. On one hand, we have the Mega-Machine, which provides the dream, but wipes out all other players. That won't work. On the other hand, we have the *Small Potatoes*, which makes a lot of people happy in a small way, but makes no one happy in a big way. That wouldn't work as people play the slots with the dream of a big win.

The *Mega-Machine* and the *Small Potatoes* are not based on actual machines, they are only examples to illustrate how the payback schedule affects a player's chances of winning.

The *Roll 'em* machine, on the other hand, is based on realistic machines that you'll find out in the market today (though the overall payback shown here is a little tight for serious play). The big incentive is still there, but at the same time, the little guys can grind away with lots of small wins while hoping for the bigger one.

Pros and Cons of Playing the Mega-Progressives

As you've seen above, in an extreme example that is not based on actual paybacks for the big mega-progressives, you'll win less often by going for a monster progressive jackpot, and overall, you'll lose more. The big progressives will give you a decent overall return while you try for the big lucky break, thus keeping you marginally happy, perhaps enough to keep playing. But you won't win as often or potentially as much as you might on the other machines available to you.

In general, the larger the progressive type jackpot, the greater the percentage of money will be withheld to make up for the big winner. In plain English, that means that the larger the Progressive type, the more money you'll lose. Part of your winning pool is going into the gigantic jackpot on these machines, and if you're not the one hitting that jackpot, than you're the one paying for it.

I used the word "type" above when describing the Progressives, because the return percentage on smaller wins for mega progressives such as Quartermania and Megabucks is not adjusted as the jackpots grow, nor do they get better for the player when the jackpots are smaller. However, while a blanket statement can't cover all situations, you would expect that more modest progressives would provide the player with a better short term return.

Let's look first at the reasons for *not* playing a Mega-Progressive.

First, you're going to lose more money, on average, at these machines, often, a lot more. Your bankroll will be drained much faster. As far as I'm concerned, that's never a good strategy. You want your bankroll to hold firm and tight, and to get as much play out of your money as possible. You also want to give yourself the best chances of winning. Sometimes, you'll be putting in coins as fast as the casino can eat them, without the casino being as reciprocal as you would like. That's a big downside to the mega progressive.

The second reason, also very important in my eyes, is to maximize your action at the machines so that you can earn the benefits afforded you by participation in the slots clubs. For me, that should be part of your winning strategy. That $100 will go a lot longer with less of an edge against it.

I'm a big believer that hitting the "free buffet" spin, or "free or discounted room" spin, or "cash rebate" spin, or any of the other prizes given to slots players who show enough action, is well worth considering as part of your winnings. The smaller the cost to get to comp-land, the better off you are. It's more fun to talk about the fun when the steak and lobster is on the house.

Now, I'll explain the reason that you might want to pay for the mega-progressives. The gravitational pull of multi-million dollar jackpots is just too much to resist, even at the cost of some percentage points in return. For many, that's the whole point of playing the slot machines in the first place.

With a lot of luck and the right timing, one pull can change your life. Whether it is the lottery, or the big progressives, the attraction of one stroke in time changing everything is certainly something to think about.

I've told you the good and bad about these big boys. It's your call now. I always like to go for the best odds, because that gives you the best chances of winning. And I like spending as little as I can to earn my comps. Personally, I'm not a dreamer. But it's your money and your dreams. If your goal is to try for that long shot, may the gods of luck be with you.

WINNING STRATEGY #11

Playing Small Progressives

Playing smaller progressives is a much smarter percentage play than the larger progressives. Since less money is being taken out to feed the progressive than the mega progressives, you'll get more "play" out of the machines. This is a move I like a lot better than getting drained by a big linked jackpot.

WINNING STRATEGY #12

General Progressive Strategy

Progressive jackpots are a dynamic thing. They go up and up when they haven't been hit, much like the lottery, and then get reset after they do get hit.

When you're in a casino that has a bunch of progressive jackpot banks, always play the machines hooked up to bank with the highest jackpot. I don't know how many times I've seen short-sighted players dropping coins in a progressive machine, when a similar machine several banks away, or even one bank away, contained a much higher jackpot.

With all things being equal, you should always play for the bigger money. This is a very important winning tip for progressive players.

One more thing: Always play the maximum number of coins at a progressive. Anything less, and you can't win the big jackpot.

WINNING STRATEGY #13

Tournament Strategy

One way to maximize your return at the slot machines is through tournaments. While a full discussion of tournaments is beyond the scope of this book, a few items are worth noting. If you are a tournament player, you'll want to pick the tournaments that give you the best return for the dollar invested, not only in terms of prize money, but in the comps the casino is willing to give you as part of the tournament package.

By picking and choosing between tournaments, you can find attractive packages that fit your needs like a glove. Sometimes, when you add up all the benefits to the prize money offered, you find yourself with a really sweet deal. As a member of a slots club, the casinos will keep you well informed of their tournament schedules. You can also get on the list of other casinos, or check the gambling magazines for ads advertising upcoming tournaments. The best way to find out about tournaments, however, is to get on the mailing lists.

WINNING STRATEGY #14

Finding the Loosest and Tightest Slots in a Casino.

The placement of loose and tight slot machines, and the actual paybacks of a casino's slot machines are about the closest kept secrets in a casino. Neither the slots hosts, change girls, or slots manager *know* the percentages of any of the machines, or where the best ones are located.

Through watching the machines over time, and getting to see how a machine behaves, the slots changers get to know which machines pay best, and which are the worst. However, this is only through observation. The one or two management personnel who know what is what, keep tight-lipped about the whole thing, and to nary a soul do they whisper these secrets.

I do know that side by side the loose machines there are tight machines and average machines, all mixed together, so that the casino can extract its maximum profits where possible. The loose machines serve the purpose of generating excitement, the tight machines try to extract a larger winning percentage, and the average machines do a little of both.

Despite what you might hear otherwise, there is a well-thought out strategy on where to best position one's loosest slot machines, where the medium payers should go, and where the tight machines, the one's that hold the highest house edge, are best positioned.

Casinos take their slots profits seriously, as well they should. Don't assume the casinos are dumb. Look at what Vegas has become; it's hardly the product of foolish businessmen.

Machines are not placed haphazardly. Slot machine placement is a carefully thought-out science. The profits from the slot machines account for most of a typical casino's income, and it is up to the slots director to decide how to maximize those profits.

Again, ignore what you might read in other books or hear from uninformed players. Slot machine placement is a carefully strategized art with a goal of maximizing profits. If you can get into a casino's mindset, and do some good thinking, it will open up some clues on machine placement.

The first thing you need to understand is the thinking behind placing a slots machine. The cardinal rule in attracting slots players to the machines is to get them excited. Bang, bang, clank, clank. If coins are pouring out and bells and whistles are trumpeting from winning machines, you can be sure adrenaline is flowing through the veins of the players in the slots area.

Casinos want to place the loose machines in visible areas where players are in a position to stay and play, as opposed to drop and run. Thus, central areas *within* a slots pit, like a corner machine visible from several aisles where the slots players are, may be a good spot for a loose machine. The loose machines will be sprinkled throughout strategic areas, so the excitement of frequent winners can spread throughout the slots area and keep interest high.

On the other hand, aisle machines facing out from the slots area, while visible, may tend to attract drop and run players. Machines facing table games run into similar difficulties. Winning machines won't get players motivated to leave the tables since these players tend not to be slots players. Passers-by are going elsewhere and probably won't get excited enough by a winning machine to invest hours of play. For that we need a well-placed machine deep in the slots trenches amongst the serious players. Thus, machines facing table games are generally set tighter and will pay poorly.

Slot machines facing open aisles also tend to be tighter for the simple reason that regular players do not like to sit with their back to people walking by. It's less private, and certainly less relaxing. Within a slots area is a more comfortable place to relax and play for hours. Regulars are surrounded by their own. Since regular players avoid these open aisles, areas where it's more likely that casual players may drop in coins, the machines are set tighter.

The worst machines will generally be found along the buffet and restaurant lines, waiting areas for the show, and other like areas. The players who tend to drop coins in these machines often do so to kill time.

If you're a frequent player to a slots area, you'll begin to notice which machines seem to be better. If they seem to be better machines, that is looser, they most probably are.

The best way to determine the machines that seem to be kicking up the most action, however, is by asking the change girls who have nothing to do but watch players and machines, day after day, night after night. They will notice the better machines. Ask them nicely, and you may get a great tip that will put you real close to a 99% paybacker.

Does this give us definitive information on which machines in particular are actually the best to play? No, but it does give us some clues to work with. We know to avoid the machines in the areas we've identified as most likely to contain tight machines. That's a start. And while we know that loose machines aren't identified in the casinos, the more frequent winnings associated with certain machines will become obvious over time by either your own careful observation, or that of regular players or casino slot employees we could ask. And once we got that figured out, if we can, your chances of winning become greatly improved.

Tip

Rarely will loose machines be set side by side. Casinos are aware that slots players often play in pairs, and know that the excitement from one machine can carry over to the player in the adjacent machine. Thus, machines adjacent to loose machines tend to be tight. When you do discover a loose machine, you'll want to avoid the machines on either side. See Strategy #16.

WINNING STRATEGY #15

Getting an Actual Advantage at the Machines

If you play things right, you may at times have the actual advantage, or close to it, if the full effective value of the comps are added in to the house edge. That's right, when all is said and done, you can at times find a situation that actually gives you the edge at slots! Amazing, but true.

Let's say you take advantage of one of your slots clubs with an aggressive slots player program. They run a big promotion with all sorts of goodies, cash rebates, and loose machines. You show up at the casino, grab the comp or discounted rooms, sit down to a free buffet with your companion, and after three trips to the food line and one to the desert bar (about three trips too many) you head over to the machines.

The casino has spiced the floor with some 99+% payback slot machines, and using my techniques, you nab one and settle in for some serious play. You enter your card into the machine and start racking up some playing time. The machine is hot, but you keep cool with the drinks. A friendly cocktail waitress takes interest in your play and seems to be by frequently. That's good, the drinks are cool, and they're flowing. You start with a cold iced soda, grab a few brews, and perhaps sweeten things up with a piña colada to put your mind on a tropical island.

Credits are racking up and bells are going off. You're really having a time, so much so, that after a bunch of hours have passed and your companion says it's time for the comped show, you realize that the two hours that went by fast were really four and half, a mini-marathon session at the slots.

A great show with two complimentary drinks, a few more hours at the machines, this time with some losses, but adding the end result to the afternoon session, you're still a few hundred ahead. You've done a little better than your expected 1% loss, a good day indeed, but you have really scored on the incentive program. You've racked up the action for the casino, earned a full 1% rebate (putting you right at the 100% expectancy - no casino advantage), plus piled on the comps — tee shirts, deck of cards and dice, more free meals and rooms, another show — and more.

Yes, not a bad day at all.

When you add that all up, you've done really well, and have even enjoyed the edge when all the benefits are given their full value. You've had a great time, have made the casino happy with your play (good for more stuff), and pretty much played for free.

Now, things won't always be quite this rosy but if you stick to loose machines, and practice smart money management principles, even if you're down some, you've given the casino a good game and done just what you love to do - play the slots. At the same time, you've reaped all the benefits of the slots club and planted seeds for the next trip.

Win or lose, the casino is happy with your play. The buffet lines might cost them a few dollars per head on average, and the room may be a third the stated price when all the overhead is taken into account. But they'll have a happy player who enjoyed the stay and the play, and most likely, will come back again.

And for you, the recipient of these comps, you're getting the full value of what you would have to pay as an outsider. And that's a benefit you should add to your total costs.

WINNING STRATEGY #16

Avoid Neighbors of Hot Machines

Casinos are well aware of the tendency of slots players who travel to casinos together, to naturally play side-by-side at adjacent machines. While on a social level this is, of course, fun and preferable, for serious players looking to get the best odds possible at the slots, this is a poor strategy, and will work against the goal of trying to maximize your winnings.

Knowing that players will tend to congregate around hot machines, or that friends will sit next to friends, casinos strategically position the cold potatoes next to the hot potatoes. Thus, in actual slots floor plans, you'll rarely find two high percentage payback machines as immediate neighbors. The casinos use these loose slots as bait to attract attention to the area, and as we know, winning machines always attract attention and action.

Slots managers are very aware of this psychology, and in their floor design, they position the loose slot machines, the ones we want to play, in carefully calculated positions throughout the casino. (Earlier, I talked about some of the better and worse spots within a casino, and I refer you there for those winning tips.) In smart casino design, one of the guiding principles is to spread the winning sounds, the banging of coins into the well, and all the hubbub of winning slots around the slots pit to keep the excitement all over the place and keep the players playing.

Casinos are willing to make a smaller cut on the loose machines that benefit the player, because, after all, the little extra they pay out by making one machine loose and getting the area excited, they make right back by tightening up on the two machines next to it. One hand feeds the other, so to speak.

We can take advantage of this knowledge by avoiding machines placed next to hot machines. When you see a machine paying off like crazy, and unfortunately, you're not the one for whom those bells are tolling, avoid those adjacent machines. They'll be colder than mother-in-laws.

WINNING STRATEGY #17

Play Single Machines Only

There is nothing like bells, whistles, eruptions, and noises emanating from a hot slot machine, or a bunch of hot slot machines, to generate excitement and electricity to all casino patrons within earshot of the racket, and to get them thinking that they too want to play and win.

The sounds of winning are contagious in the slots areas; the more players hear the sounds of winning, the greater the draw it is for players and non-players alike to want to get in on the action. They're thinking, "the machines are hot and paying," and instinctually park themselves in front of a machine and take their chances.

The conclusion to this train of thought is that in order to have the best chance of being a winner, *you must play only one machine at a time*. You cannot afford to lose the extra percentage points you gain by finding and playing a hot, paying machine, by handing those winning coins right back to the tight machine situated next to it. That is not a good approach. Play one machine only!

WINNING STRATEGY #18

Riding a Hot Streak

There is one principle that applies to almost all gambling games, and certainly is true at the slots: Never leave a winning machine to test out another. When you've got a great machine going, you would be crazy to walk away — even for a minute.

It wouldn't take but a few seconds from the time you got up from your seat before another savvy player zoomed in on that nest egg like a mother hen, clucking away as the payouts continued. A hot machine means a loose machine, and the percentages that this machine was set at won't change in the middle of your session. They'll be exactly the same.

WINNING STRATEGY #19

Playing Non-Progressive Slots that Just Hit the Jackpot

Many players feel that a machine that has just been hit for a big winner is no longer due, and should be avoided like the plague. No way, Jose. Slot machines have no memory, and are set to completely random standards. Every spin is completely independent of the spin before it. It is just like a pair of dice. The dice don't remember that a seven was just rolled, and thus the chances of another seven being rolled is the same as it always was, and always will be, one chance in six.

While slot machines are certainly more "intelligent" than a pair of dice, being equipped with computer chips, this processing power is used only to allow random spins for each time the reels are set in motion. There is no preset order of winning combinations, or trigger that sets in motion a different combination possibility based on whether the last spin was a winner or a loser. It is random every time the reels are spun.

Therefore, a machine hits the jackpot on spin one, doesn't lessen the chances one iota that it won't hit that same jackpot combination on spin two. At the same time, it doesn't increase the odds either, but the point is this: You've got a hot machine that is spewing out winners. That's what you look for in a casino.

Of course, if you're done gambling for a while, hitting a jackpot is a perfect time to take a break; what better excuse? But if you're still geared for action, why walk from the horse that brought you through the pearly gates?

WINNING STRATEGY #20

Playing Progressive Slots that Just Hit the Jackpot

In the above example, we talked about hitting the big payout on a machine that was hot, and sticking with that machine if you were still in the gambling mood. But that was for non-progressive machines.

With progressive machines, it is an entirely different strategy that we will pursue. Once a progressive jackpot is hit, whether that jackpot is linked to other machines in the casino, throughout a larger jurisdiction, or even resides solely on the machine itself, than you must immediately call it quits with the machine you're playing, and with any other machine that is linked up to that progressive system.

Your average percentage payback in slots, what we refine into the terms "loose" or "tight," is dependent on the payback chart listed on the machine itself.

To use an easy example, let's take 100 coins, paint sixty of them red, thirty-nine of them green, and one of them blue. If we pick a coin blindly from the mix and it is green, we win $1, if it is blue, $20, and if it is red, we *lose* $1. Every time we finish picking we throw the coin back in the mix and try again.

This analogy is pretty close to what actually occurs with slots payouts, only in this simple example, there are only two winning combinations, the green and blue, not ten or twenty as we might find at an actual machine.

Let's examine what the chances of winning are. Thirty-nine green coins will pay us one dollar each for a total of $39. One blue coin will pay us $20. We have a total of $59 we can win against $60 we could lose. Overall, out of every hundred coins picked, at one dollar each, the expectation would be for a $1 loss. That translates to a 1% house edge, what I would call a very loose machine.

Let's now presume that this is a progressive game, and since the blue coin hadn't been picked in a while, it had risen to the high value of a twenty coin payout, from its original starting payout of ten coins. On your next pick, bingo, you get the blue coin and get paid $20 for your good luck.

Great, let's say you're up $15 in the game now, but since the blue coin, the "progressive" was hit, the winning combination is now down to a ten coin payout.

This changes *everything*. Let's examine what your payback percentage would be. Your odds of winning are still exactly the same as before; but your payouts for these wins are not! Thirty-nine greens pays us $39 as before, sixty reds lose us $60, also as before, but the blue, now pays only $10. The winning combinations total $49, the losing combinations total $60, for an expected net loss on every hundred picks of $11, or an 11% house edge. This is not a loose slots at all. Whereas before you had a great game going, giving you just a 1% nut to crack, you'll now be losing big at this progressive game.

This illustrates the difference between your chance of hitting a winner, what is called your *hit frequency*, or *frequency of winning*, as opposed to your *payback percentage* — quite different concepts. Your frequency of winning didn't change after the blue coin was picked. There were still forty ways to win (thirty-nine greens and one blue), and sixty ways to lose (the sixty reds). Your frequency of winning here is 40%, which is much higher than you would find at an average machine, especially a progressive.

The payback percentage, as I showed above, has taken a drastic discount, because your jackpot (which has a frequency of occurrence of one in a hundred, or 1%) is worth only ten coins, not twenty as before. Your game went from being very good, to very poor.

Going back to real life slots, this is the exact principle that applies to your machines. Your frequency of winning doesn't change just because the jackpot was hit, nor for that matter, does your chances of hitting that jackpot on the next spin. But the problem is that your percentage payback has dropped like a stone over the abyss, and you're getting terrible odds.

Thus, as I said earlier, you want to stay away from progressives that have just been hit, and conversely play ones that are hanging like ripe fruit with big payouts to the lucky winner.

Winning Jackpots

Every slots player's dream is to hit the monster jackpot. In fact, as more and more machines are linked together by big companies such as IGT, these jackpots get bigger and bigger, and more and more players get quite interested in taking a crack at it.

Well, what if you get lucky? Here's what you can expect. First of all, the casino will probably want to verify that the jackpot was struck legitimately. With all the crooks and angle players out there, the casino runs a constant battle to make sure that big wins are on the up and up.

You'll need to fill out some forms for the IRS and show ID for verification. If your heart is racing wildly from the win, you'll have to do your best to calm down to get the formalities over with.

Most big jackpots will be paid out over 20 years in equal payments. Other jackpots may be paid in one lump sum, or a combination of large partial sums. How you will get paid depends upon the sponsoring company of the jackpot. (Usually it is not the casino running the progressive, but a large slots manufacturer such as IGT or Bally's). It's really not something you need to worry about until it happens.

You also have a choice on whether you want to remain anonymous or allow the casino to use the event to get publicity. If you want to be in the spotlight for a little bit, you can have some fun with this. The downside though, be forewarned, is that you might get bombarded by investment advisors and salesmen of every ilk including con artists, all of whom are trying to help you spend your money. Long lost friends, and ones not so long lost, might emerge out of the closet hoping you'll loan some of the loot since you're so rich now. Hey, not everything is perfect.

In any case, if you do win the big one, you can start attending to your dreams. Life is about to get better.

Winning Summary

The key to beating the slots, as in all gambling pursuits, is to play only the machines that give you the best chances of winning. Your chances of coming out ahead at the slots are in direct proportion to the payout percentage. The greater the payout percentage, the better chance you have of walking away with a profit.

For example, a machine that pays back 99% gives you a very good chance of riding just a little luck into profits. On the other hand, a machine that pays only 50%, will take your money so fast that you'll need a lot more than luck to get ahead. A house edge of 50% is just too steep. But that's not the norm you'll face. In slots-friendly casinos in Las Vegas and Atlantic City you'll generally be playing in the mid to upper 90's. That gives you a decent shot, certainly a whole lot better than you'll find at the airport.

We've gone over all the winning techniques and secrets in this chapter, how to find the best paying machines, how to manage your money, and many other important concepts. It's now up to you to play smart and be a winner.

Jackpots and Taxes

Before I begin this chapter, let me alert you to the fact that I am neither an accountant, a lawyer, nor an expert on tax law. If indeed you do manage to win a jackpot, you will be best served by hiring competent help to determine the proper reporting of gambling income and deductions to the IRS or other tax body that may apply. In other words, while on your jackpot vacation, don't use my advice as your final source; peel off a bill or two and give it to the pros. I've provided some very general guidelines below.

Casinos are required by law to ensure that any single slot machine payout of $1,200 or over is reported to the Internal Revenue Service. A W-2G tax form must immediately be completed by the $1,200 winner at the casino. This form will be quickly forwarded to the IRS.

The W-2G form is comparable to the W-2 form you receive from your employer. The W-2 verifies the amount of money you have made in any given period of time, while the W-2G validates the money you received in slot machine winnings. The total dollar amount on the W-2G is added to your earnings on your W-2 form to determine your total taxable income for the year.

For example, if your annual household income is $30,000 and you won $2,000 playing the slots, your total taxable income for the year would increase to $32,000.

Two valid forms of identification must be made available to the casino at the time of any win. These might include a driver's license, credit card, or social security card.

The government allows slot machine gamblers to deduct losses up to, but not exceeding, the amount won. If you won a $2,000 jackpot in one year playing the slots, but lost a miscellaneous total of $2,500 in that same year, you would not be able to take the $500 difference as a loss off of your taxes.

The losses to be offset against winnings can't be subtracted directly from the itemized winnings; they must be taken separately as a miscellaneous deduction. This way the government is able to see exact winnings and exact losses. Losses from the previous year will not be accepted as losses for the present year. If that $2,500 loss had come from the previous year's play, you would be unable to deduct it against the current year's $2,000 win.

If you win a jackpot under $1,200, the casino is not required to report your winnings.

Keeping Logbooks

If you're a serious player, it is important to keep itemized logs of daily amounts won and lost at the slot machines — so that if you do win a jackpot, you can offset the jackpot total against all the losses it took to get you there. Dates, times and places are important to include in these journals. Keeping the names of any employees or witnesses who are able to verify your losses might be helpful. All of this may seem tedious, but when forced to deal with the Internal Revenue Service, your records can never be too detailed.

A simple way to tally daily wins and losses is to carry a small notebook, diary, or journal. This will make it easy for you to jot down information as you play. If someone is playing with you, both of you may want to take turns recording necessary information. All transactions should be accounted for after each gambling session. The more verification you have of loss deductions, the more substantial and acceptable your loss claims will be.

Even if you're only playing casually, it may be wise to keep at least an informal record, as you never know when you might hit the jackpot. It will also let you know, in black and white, how you have done at the machines.

Sometimes the IRS demands additional evidence for gambling losses. These might include airline tickets, hotel bills, gas receipts or signed documents from witnesses who are able to verify your losses. Witnesses could be other players, the change persons, slots hosts, or a casino supervisor. If you do hit the jackpot, the time put into this documentation will be well worth the trouble.

Slots club players may also get loss documentation from the casinos. Their sophisticated tracking systems keep tally of everything — hours played, amount of coins bet, wins and losses, coin denominations — all for the purpose of tracking your action and giving you comps for your good play. If you nail a jackpot or two, this documentation is indisputable evidence for your claim. Again, you will need to seek competent tax advice from a professional should you hit some big wins, and expecially if you hit a monster jackpot.

Money Management & Winning

Managing your money is the first step toward being a winning player. Piling up several hundred dollars on a hot streak means nothing if you immediately turn around and give it straight back to the house.

A player that consistently gives his winnings back to the casino is a player that doesn't give himself a chance to win — in a sense, a player who *refuses* to win. No matter how well a session is going, this player feels the need to keep playing until his or her money is gone. This player I describe is a loser. Only an unusually long winning streak or a monster jackpot can put this player into the win column. This type of player plays as if the goal is to lose — and if he can't lose it today, there's always tomorrow. For players hell-bent on losing, it doesn't take long for the odds to cooperate.

Losing is not what this book is about. I'm trying to teach you how to win. Part of this formula involves the use of the winning techniques and strategies described throughout this book. Another part, the most important part, is money management. If you don't handle your money with an intelligent plan from the start, you're going to come out a loser every time.

Money management has several aspects:

Five Money Management Principles

First and foremost is having a *winning attitude*. To be a winner, you have to *genuinely want to be a winner*.

Second, you must *play within your means*. We'll discuss bankroll considerations and optimal bet size for your bankroll in a moment. We'll also continue this discussion in setting loss limits.

Third, you need to *protect your winning streaks*. We've talked a lot about restricting losses; this section shows you how to keep the winnings. There are some basic principles that must always be followed.

Fourth, you have to have *emotional control*. You must be able to control yourself at the machines and not let yourself be overwhelmed by the gambling atmosphere.

Fifth and finally, money management is all about *setting limits*. You can never allow yourself to take such a beating at the machines that you not only ruin your vacation, but lose more money than you can afford to lose.

Let's look at each of these money management elements in turn. I'll begin with the winning attitude.

First: The Winning Attitude

I am continually amazed by the number of slots players who always manage to lose during their trips to Las Vegas, Atlantic City, on the riverboats and Indian reservations, the Bahamas, and all the other gambling meccas around the world. And it's not just slots players. I see blackjack and craps players, poker players, video poker and roulette players, basically, gamblers of all stripes consistently losing because they don't come into the casinos with a winning attitude.

Does a good attitude affect the odds of the games or the machines? No. Whether you're the happiest camper on earth, or are the sorriest loser this side of suckersville, the odds are the same. The slot machines won't care how you feel because they won't know. If you and I sit down to pull the handle for 10 spins each, it won't matter which one of us pushes the button and sets the reels in motion. The result will be the same, regardless of your mood or whatever your horoscope says.

Despite all of this, how you feel definitely does affect your overall chances of winning. A player that goes into the casino with the goal of winning, does everything he or she can do to achieve that goal. This gambler will closely follow the money management advice we lay down in this section. That's the mark of a winner. They'll play within their means, they'll set reasonable limits, they'll control themselves at the machines, and when they're winning big, the casinos will see their back at the cashier's cage, converting the winnings into cash.

The loser, on the other hand, will do everything wrong. From the outside, they will appear as if they are actually trying to lose. Losers have losing written all over them; in their actions, their moods, and of course, their results. No crowbar will pry these players away from the machines or tables until they've managed to lose their money. We've all seen plenty of these players. I've seen and heard enough stories myself to fill an encyclopedia.

To be sure, the casinos hold the edge at the slots and in many places a substantial edge. But players can still win, that is, the *smart* players can. Follow the advice in this section, and you'll be smart too, the one gambler the casinos don't feast on; you'll feast on them instead.

The next stop in money management is figuring out the correct bankroll for *you*, and playing within those limits.

Second: Bankrolling – Play Within Your Means

Determining the correct bankroll for you as a player is not just about the money you can afford to risk at the tables from a financial point of view; it's also about what you can afford to lose emotionally. There is no rule more important in all of gambling.

The possibilities of taking a loss are real, and if that loss will hurt, you're playing like a fool. It is inevitable that players who gamble over their heads will lose more than they can afford. Luck won't help these players because even when the good music comes their way, as it surely will, they won't quit while they're ahead. They keep on going and going and going until the inevitable occurs.

By definition, the player that loses when he bets too much is getting hurt. Don't let that player be you. Gambling with needed funds is a foolish gamble. However, if you never play over your head, you'll never suffer.

Luck fluctuates in gambling. Sometimes you win, sometimes you lose. However, the goal for the intelligent gambler is to protect themselves in the times they lose and that means to set loss limits, not only for a particular session, but for an entire trip as well.

Let's go over some basic bankrolling principles.

Session Bankroll

The amount of money that you bring to the machines should be able to afford you two things: 1. The ability to handle a moderate size losing streak, and 2. A large amount of playing time to allow your luck to turn itself around and maybe swing your fortune in the other direction. That amount, which we'll discuss in a second, will be your one session stake. The rule is this: if that stake gets drained, you call it a day.

The key concept in formulating single session bankrolls for a machine is to restrict losses to affordable amounts. That's why when I discuss bringing money to a machine, I say to bring "moderate" amounts, not substantial amounts. *Minimizing* losses is the key. You can't always win. That's a fact of life for gamblers. If you're losing, keep the losses affordable - take a break. Don't let yourself get caught in a situation where you get beat badly. There's always another day.

You should have enough money at the machines to cover 200 plays. A *play* is the amount of money you'll be betting on one spin. For example, if you're playing 25¢ machines and are playing three coins at a time, your play costs 75¢. Thus, your bankroll for the session should be $150. If your coin instead was $1, then you would need a $600 machine stake (200 plays x $3). 5¢ players would bring $30 at three coins per spin. These are the maximum numbers. You can risk less, which you might want to do anyway.

These conservative numbers are designed to keep your losses to affordable amounts. This doesn't mean that you'll lose the

amounts shown above, only that *you won't lose more than that.*
That's a big step in the right direction right there.

Trip Bankroll

A trip to a casino is really a multitude of individual sessions. For
short trips, like a weekend jaunt, you may want to have enough to
cover three to five sessions, for longer trips, say up to a week or
two, five to seven sessions. The whole purpose of the trip bankroll
is to have enough money to keep you playing, even though you
may be having a particularly bad run of luck, and at the same
time, to restrict your overall losses to "acceptable" amounts.

That's why I take such a conservative approach. By avoiding
overbetting, you give yourself the opportunity to bounce back
after bad luck. You also avoid wiping out your one session stake
or, even worse, digging deeper and deeper into your funds and
running the risk of being totally destroyed.

Thus, using the figures worked out above, with three coins average per play, 25¢ players should bring $450-$750, depending
upon the number of sessions they plan to play, $1 players should
bring $1,800-$3,000, and 5¢ players, $90-$150.

These bankroll amounts allow you to withstand any normal losing streak and still have the resources to play more and bounce
back on top. If the numbers scare you, then you need to think
about lower denomination machines. Money can be lost quickly
at the machines — you probably know this as well as I do. It's
better to play it safe.

Third: Protect Your Winning Streaks

Once you've accumulated a sizable win at the slot machines, and have had yourself a good run, the most important thing is to walk away a winner. There is no worse feeling than skulking away from a machine after having lost back all of your wins.

The general guidelines I recommend, is to put away three fourths or more of your winnings into a "protected" area that you won't touch under any circumstances. That money is bankable, for you won't play it. Whether those wins are put aside as coins in a "no touch zone" plastic bucket, a mental note to shut off after you drop to a certain number of credits, or however you do it, *make sure you it gets done.*

Never touch the money you've set aside in your protected zone. Never. Protecting your wins is just as important as limiting your losses. Once the coins or credits are on your side, it's your money, not the casinos. It's yours now. You risked and you won. Great. Now take it home with you and do something fun with it.

For example, let's say you're up $200 after a pretty good session at the $1 slots. Put $150 of that money into your protected zone. Play out the remaining $50. This doesn't mean you have to lose the $50 if things turn sour; you can call it quits after $25 has been bet off of that, guaranteeing yourself an extra $25 win! But, in any case, don't dip below the $50. If that extra buffer is gone, you're gone, a definite loser.

Keep playing with the rest of your winnings, putting more aside as the wins accumulate. By doing this, your guaranteed winning pile steadily increases. Ride the cycle upwards. If the $200 mushrooms to $350, now move your protected zone to $300 in winnings and play with the extra $50. If your bankroll still increases with more wins, put more aside again.

Once the winning streak stops and the tides of fortune turn against you, it's time to leave the table — a guaranteed winner who can look back on that profitable session with great satisfaction.

Set no limits on a winning streak. When you've got a hot hand, ride it for all its worth. And when things cool down, chill yourself out with a cool drink down by the music lounge.

Fourth: Emotional Control

Astute gamblers have one thing in common — they know how to manage their money and keep cool in the thick of the casino, whether they're up and riding high, or struggling against a cold machine with the worst of luck. Superior playing skills alone does not make one a winning player. The concept here is self control: the ability of a player to keep the game in check and never lose sight of the winning strategies.

Winning and losing streaks are a very real part of playing the slots. It is how you deal with the inherent ups and downs at the machines that determines just how well you will fare at your sessions.

We're all going to lose sometimes. We're also going to win sometimes. It is the smart gambler, the one keeping it all under control, that will win big when he's winning, and minimize losses when he's losing. It's all about emotional control. You can't change the spins on the reel. You can however, change your reactions to them.

I'll show a simple example of how a loss of emotional control can quickly change a big winning session into a disaster. Let's say a bettor starts out with a bankroll of $200 and has been playing 25¢ machines. After two hours of tough play, he has ridden a surge of luck to $225 in winnings. Now he has $425 in front of him.

Getting greedy and caught up in the excitement of the game, the gambler now really wants to put the squeeze on, so he goes against his pre-planned strategy, if he even has one, and now goes for the $1 machines. With a little luck and a few big wins in a row, he's on easy street.

After a bunch of losses, he gets frantic, and goes for two machines at a time, pushing all his money out there. And now, more bad luck. Suddenly, a careful strategy that netted $225 got transformed into "if I can get lucky on this play, please" strategy. No surprise, the player loses all the original stake. It's madness.

That's one side of the equation. Thankfully, there are more inspiring tales that we can profitably learn from.

Let me tell you about an elderly couple I met on one of my trips to Vegas. This was my first trip back since they built the latest round of resort-casinos, New York, New York, Monte Carlo, and others. I was checking out the latest in casino design, and of course, the slot machines, to see what the new trends were. While wandering around a particularly lively bank of slots, I ran into a couple, Bob and Maryanne, and got to shooting the breeze with them a bit.

They had been coming to Las Vegas for 30 years and had been regular slots players all that time. As it turns out, they had once been blackjack players as well for a while and had bought my book more than fifteen years ago. While they had some success at the twenty-one tables, the game couldn't hold their fancy. At heart, then and now, as they explained, they were dedicated slots players. They had played nothing else for the last 10 years. They loved the relaxation of the game — the fact that they could play the machines at their own pace, with no dealer to hurry them along.

While Maryanne was mostly holding her own that day, Bob was really on a roll, and had already won $600 at the $1 slots. He was hoping to get up to $750, and then $1,000. The machine had been kind, and with a cold beer in his hand and two comp tickets to the dinner buffet stuffed into his back pocket, life was good. Bob's luck went up and down, and his bankroll slipped about a hundred as we spoke.

This was to be their last day before they flew back to their home in New Iberia, Louisiana (home of the Tabasco company), and they were hoping to ride out of town feeling extra good.

As I was watching, Bob almost caught the big one. The first two reels lined up like a dream, and the third, barely missing, made the spin a loser. Had it lined up for Bob, he would have won the big jackpot. He got a kick out of that and said to me, "I've seen more of them than you can shake a stick at. Well that's it pod'ner. $500 is a good day. See you around." With that, Bob and Mary-anne cashed out, and arm and arm took off for the cashier's cage and, presumably, the beginning of a good evening.

It was what I love to see; people playing to win and playing to have fun. Bob and Maryanne knew when to get up and walk away with their winnings.

Fifth: Setting Limits

This is really a continuation of the discussion on bankrolling; keep in mind that when the discussion concerns some aspect of money management, everything is interrelated. You always want to set a limit on losses so that one bad session doesn't devastate you, and at the same time, a "stop-loss" on winnings as well, so that once you have a good win going, you never give the casino a chance to get it back.

Before sitting at the table and making your bets, you must decide on the amount of money you'll stake. You must restrict your losses to that amount only, should luck turn against you. If you refuse to go against this rule you can never take a serious beating. If things go poorly at first, take a break — remarkably, it's as simple as that.

Remember, when you're winning big, put a substantial chunk of these winnings in a "do not touch" pile, and play with the rest. You never want to hand your winnings back to the casino. Should a losing streak occur, get out of there — a winner!!!

Never risk needed money at the machines no matter how lucky you feel. Just as many "lucky" players contributed to the phenomenal growth of casinos as unlucky players. Well, perhaps there were, in fact, far more of the latter, but you get the point. The reality of gambling is that money can be lost, and if that money is earmarked for rent or food, or any other necessity in your life, you're making a whopping mistake.

I know this is all common sense, but it bears repeating because so many players go against this basic rule. There's an old Las Vegas saying about a guy who rides into town in a $20,000 Cadillac and leaves in a $100,000 Greyhound bus. Unfortunately, that saying bears a lot of truth. The list of sad stories from out of control gamblers is virtually unending. And more can get added every day, lots more.

Let's say you're a quarter player and are on a winning streak that has expanded your starting machine bankroll for the day from $100 to $350, a nice $250 win. Should you go up to the $1 machine to really go for the kill? Absolutely not. You're hot and you're winning. The action is good. But raising your stake to the $1 machines now magnifies all the bets. Sure you can win a lot more. But don't let greed lead you astray. Greed nabs most gamblers and the end result is an unhappy player who got buried by that greed.

After a session of doing well at the slots, all that's needed for the winds of fortune to change is a short losing streak at a higher level. You can quickly wipe out *all* of your winnings *at a level of play uncomfortable to you*. This momentum can escalate rapidly when greed has overcome sanity. In such situations, people often dig deep quickly — thus digging themselves into an often inescapable hole. Not good. No one can afford to play at a level that jeopardizes so much so quickly. Betting over your head spells danger.

So many gamblers follow this pattern that I honestly wonder where their goals really are. Are they really trying to win, or are they raising the stakes for nothing more than the adrenaline rush? They'll win say $300, bump up the money (it could be the slots, the table games or any other gamble), and if they don't get wiped out at the higher level, they may win again, and bump up the stakes one more time. Well, it catches up quickly. Eventually, luck will turn. It always does. If these players were smart, they would get out while the getting was good. But inevitably, and almost invariably, they will not leave until they take the big fall.

What are these players really trying to do? The psychology on all of this is complex, but the empirical evidence is always the same. They lose it all back and more. There is almost no way that these gamblers can come out ahead because no matter how lucky they get, they raise the stakes again so that all it takes is a small losing streak to wipe it all out — their winnings, their original stake, and then in desperation, even more. I've seen it time and time again. And then these players wonder, "what happened?"

Greed happened, and a loss of control. But we can do away with these things, especially the latter, right now. Stick to the level you started at, so when you do win, you stay a winner. It's okay to reach for the stars, but don't be jumping off the bridge to catch them. Whether you win or lose at slots, always keep to the level of betting that you originally decided to play at.

Remember: You're Playing for Fun

Gambling is a form of entertainment and if you can't afford the possibility of losing — don't gamble at the stakes you were considering. Either play at lower levels or don't gamble at all. If the playing of the game becomes a cause of undue anxiety, for whatever the reason, than it ceases to be a form of entertainment and you need a break. Take some time away from the game, be it a coffee break or a month's rest.

Playing under anxiety not only ruins the fun of the game but also adversely affects play and can influence you to make decisions contrary to what smart strategy dictates.

Your goal in gambling is not just to win, but to get satisfaction out of the game. Keep that in mind and you can never go wrong.

You can't always win — even when the odds favor you — and you won't always lose, even when the odds are against you. In the short run, anything can happen and usually does. But over the long run, luck evens itself out. It is skill, in the bets one makes, and how one plays the game, that will determine if a player is a winner or a loser.

LAST SECTION

A Final Word

Well, that's about it. I've covered a lot of material in this book, and hopefully, given you a good shot at beating slot machines. You've had a chance to learn all about slot machines, from their early history, and development through the years, to the twenty winning strategies that will improve your chances of going home a winner.

I'll give you one more reminder: Always gamble sanely, and view the slots as a form of entertainment, not as a profit center. Play for as long as the machines are fun, then quit. You can never go wrong this way.

It's up to you now to follow my advice and be a winner at slots. Give 'em what for.

Avery Cardoza

Glossary

Action - The total amount of money played measured by the sum of all bets placed. Thus, betting a quarter 100 times, would be equivalent to $25.00 in *action*, or betting $1 for 700 plays adds up to $700 in *action*. Action does not take into account starting or ending bankroll, or wins or losses — just total $ bets.

Average Payer - A machine that is neither tight, nor loose, but in between.

Bank, Bank of Machines - This is a group of machines connected together in a structure as a design unit.

Bar - A popular symbol on slot machines. This symbol is often found as one bar, two bars, and three bars.

Big Bertha - The gigantic slot machines of many reels, usually eight to ten, that are strategically placed by casinos near their front entrance (usually, but not always) to lure curious players into their casinos for a pull or two.

Big Coin Machine - A slot machine requiring $5, $25, or larger coin to play.

Big Coin Player - A slots player who plays $5, $25, or larger coins.

Blanks - The stops on a reel which contain no symbols, thus, blank stops, or *blanks*.

Buy-Your-Pay - A machine with a single payout line that will only pay on certain symbols if enough coins are played.

Cage - The cashier's cage, where players can exchange chips for cash, or change traveler's checks. The cage usually won't accept large numbers of coins. That must be done at a change booth.

Change Booth - A booth set up for the specific purpose of changing players bills into coins, or their coins into bills.

Changeperson - The casino employee who services the machines area for the purpose of changing bills into coins.

Carousels - An oval or round-shaped area containing a bank of machines. A change person often sits in the center, enclosed in the space.

Cashout Button - This button, when pressed, releases all the coins that were won, or at least held by the machine.

Changeperson - The casino employee responsible for changing player bills into coins. The changeperson usually roams the slots area, though he or she may be "stationed" in a carousel.

Cherry - A popular symbol on the slot machines.

Cold - A machine that is paying out less than expected, or a player on a losing streak.

Comp - Short for *complimentary*. The freebies given out by the casino, usually as a reward for play. These can take the form of free or discounted drinks, rooms, shows, buffets and regular meals, and more.

Criss-Cross Machine - see **Five Line Criss Cross**.

Denomination - The size of coin (or bill) used to play a particular machine. 5¢, 25¢, and $1, are the most popular denominations found. Increasingly, larger denominations such as $5, $25, $100, and even higher are found now as well.

Extended Paytable - On slot machines, when the paytable showing winning combinations extends below the play buttons, on the "belly glass."

Five Line Criss Cross - A multiple payline machine that has five winning directions, three horizontal and two diagonal.

Hit Frequency - The expected frequency of winning payouts that a slot machine will produce. For example, if a winning combination will hit, on average, one time in six, the hit frequency will be 16.67%.

Hold - The percentage or actual dollar amounts a casino wins from its players. Also known as **Hold Percentage.**

Hot - A machine that is paying out better than expected, or a player on a winning streak.

Jackpot - The big win on any machine - the jackpot!

Lemon - A symbol found on slot machines.

Liberty Bell - The original slots machine invented by Charles Fey. Also, the symbol on the reels of many slot machines.

Long Run - The concept of what certain results are expected to be when occurring over many trials, thus, *in the long run.*

Loose, Loose Machine - A slot machine marked by frequent winners, with a high percentage payback to the players. This is opposed to a tight machine which has a low percentage payback.

Loose Payer - A loose machine.

Max Coin Button - The button that plays all credits allowed, usually three or five, when pushed.

Medium Coin Machine - A 50¢ or $1 denomination machine.

Medium Coin Player - A player who plays the 50¢ or $1 denomination machines.

Mega-Progressive - A super-jackpot progressive that can get as high as millions of dollars. See **Progressives.**

Mills Machines - An early machine, manufactured by Mills, an early slot innovator and producer, that was the first to use the fruit symbols and have a jackpot.

Money Management - The strategy used by smart players to wisely manage their money while gambling as to preserve their capitol, avoid big losses, and manage their wins.

Monster Jackpot - An enormous paying jackpot — what every slot player dreams about hitting.

Multiple Payline - A slot machine with more than one winning payline. Three and five payline machines are the most common. Occassionally, a manufacturer will produce other combinations into the market but none seem to have caught on as well as the standard single payline machine.

Multiple Progressives - A machine which contains more than one progressive jackpot.

Multiplier - A multiple coin slots which pays proportionately more on winning combinations for each coin played, except for the big jackpot, which when hit, typically pays a disproportionately higher total if all coins are played (to induce players to play the full number of coins) than if a lesser amount were gambled.

One-Armed Bandit - A colorful slang term used for slot machines.

One Credit Button - The button that plays one credit for the player when pushed. The spin reels button will need to be pushed afterwards to spin the reels.

Payback or Payout Percentage - The expected return percentage for money wagered. A 97% payback states that the expected return on every dollar bet will be 97¢, for a loss of 3¢.

Payline - The line on the glass over the reels of the machine, behind which the symbols need to line up to be a winning combination.

Paytable - The display on the slot machine showing winning combinations and their payouts.

Payout Meter - The display on the machine that shows the number of coins played and won on a spin.

Progressive Machines, Progressives - Progressives feature a growing jackpot which increases each time a coin is inserted into any slots machine that is hooked up to the progressive meter. When the jackpot does hit, the lucky player wins the total accumulated in the jackpot, and the jackpot total will be reset to a predetermined starting point.

Rating - The evaluation received by a player from the casino stating the level of action this player gives the casino.

Reels - The spinning mechanism containing the symbols on a slots machine. Tehnically called **Stepper Reels**.

Seven - A popular symbol on slot machines, generally showing up in the number form "7."

Short Run - A brief sequence of trials, where anything can happen, even though the odds say they may not be likely.

Single Coin Machine - A slot machine that accepts only a single coin for play. Rarely, if ever, found today.

Single Payline Machine - A slot machine with only one payline that determines winners.

Slot Machines - A mechanical or chip-driven machine that accepts bets in the form of coins or credits, spins reels, and disperses wins according to the combinations of symbols which match those as shown on a printed paytable.

Slots - Short for slot machines.

Slots Host - The person responsible for taking care of the slots players and all their needs.

Slots Palace - A casino that only contains slot machines.

Small Coin Machine - A 5¢, 10¢, or 25¢ denomination machine.

Small Coin Player - A player who plays the 5¢, 10¢, or 25¢ denomination machines.

Start - On some machines, pushing this button will spin the reels if credits are already bet.

Stepper Reels - See **Reels**.

Symbols - The various markings on a slot machine reel. The most popular are those originated by the Mills Company, which show fruits, bells and bars. However, many casinos put in their own logos for the big payouts.

Tight Machine - A slot machine marked by infrequent winners, with a low percentage payback to the players. This is opposed to a loose machine which has a high percentage payback.

Well - The bottom metal area of the machine where winning coins fall.

Wild Play Machines - A new breed of slot machines that use wild symbols to multiply the winning payouts.

Wild Symbol - The symbol earmarked as "wild" by a slot manufacturer, could be designated as any winning symbol for the benefit of the player, or in addition, can increase the normal winning payout by a multiple.

Window - The glass area in the front of the machine where the player views the symbols and reels.

GRI'S PROFESSIONAL VIDEO POKER STRATEGY
Win Money at Video Poker! With the Odds!

At last, for the **first time,** and for **serious players only,** the GRI **Professional Video Poker** strategy is released so you too can play to win! **You read it right** - this strategy gives you the **mathematical advantage** over the casino and what's more, it's **easy to learn!**

PROFESSIONAL STRATEGY SHOWS YOU HOW TO WIN WITH THE ODDS - This **powerhouse strategy,** played for **big profits** by an **exclusive** circle of **professionals,** people who make their living at the machines, is now made available to you! You too can win - with the odds - and this **winning strategy** shows you how!

HOW TO PLAY FOR A PROFIT - You'll learn the **key factors** to play on a **pro level**: which machines will turn you a profit, break-even and win rates, hands per hour and average win per hour charts, time value, team play and more! You'll also learn big play strategy, alternate jackpot play, high and low jackpot play and key strategies to follow.

WINNING STRATEGIES FOR ALL MACHINES - This **comprehensive,** advanced pro **package** not only shows you how to win money at the 8-5 progressives, but also, the **winning strategies** for 10s or better, deuces wild, joker's wild, flat-top, progressive and special options features.

BE A WINNER IN JUST ONE DAY - In just one day, after learning our strategy, you will have the skills to **consistently win money** at video poker - with the odds. The strategies are easy to use under practical casino conditions.

FREE BONUS - PROFESSIONAL PROFIT EXPECTANCY FORMULA ($15 VALUE) - For serious players, we're including this free bonus essay which explains the professional profit expectancy principles of video poker and how to relate them to real dollars and cents in your game.

To order send just $50 by check or money order to:
Cardoza Publishing, P.O. Box 1500, Cooper Station, New York, NY 10276

Win at Blackjack Without Counting Cards!!!
Multiple Deck 1, 2, 3 Non-Counter - Breakthrough in Blackjack!!!

BEAT MULTIPLE DECK BLACKJACK WITHOUT COUNTING CARDS!
You heard right! Now, for the **first time ever**, win at multiple deck blackjack **without counting cards**! Until I developed the Cardoza Multiple Deck Non-Counter (The 1,2,3 Strategy), I thought it was impossible. Don't be intimidated anymore by four, six or eight deck games - for **you have the advantage**. It doesn't matter how many decks they use, for this easy-to-use and proven strategy keeps you **winning - with the odds**!

EXCITING STRATEGY - ANYONE CAN WIN! - We're **excited** about this strategy for it allows
anyone at all, against any number of decks, to have the **advantage** over any casino in the world in a multiple deck game. You don't count cards, you don't need a great memory, you don't need to be good at math - you only need to know the **winning secrets** of the 1,2,3 Multiple Deck Non-Counter and use but a **little effort** to be a **winner**.

SIMPLE BUT EFFECTIVE! - **Now the answer is here**. This strategy is so **simple**, yet so
effective, you will be amazed. With a **minimum of effort**, this remarkable strategy, which we also call the 1,2,3 (as easy as 1,2,3), allows you to win without studiously following cards. Drink, converse with your fellow players or dealer - they'll never suspect that you can **beat the casino**!

PERSONAL GUARANTEE - And you have my personal **guarantee of satisfaction**, 100%
money back! This breakthrough strategy is my personal research and is guaranteed to give you the edge! If for any reason you're not satisfied, send back the materials unused within 30 days for a full refund.

BE A LEISURELY WINNER! - If you just want to play a **leisurely game** yet have the expectation
of winning, the answer is here. Not as powerful as a card counting strategy, but **powerful enough to make you a winner** - with the odds!!!

EXTRA BONUS! - Complete listing of all options and variations at blackjack and how they affect
the player. ($5.00 Value!)
EXTRA, EXTRA BONUS!! - Not really a bonus since we can't sell you the strategy without
protecting you against getting barred. The 1,000 word essay, **"How to Disguise the Fact That You're an Expert,"** and the 1,500 word **"How Not To Get Barred,"** are also included free. ($15.00 Value)

To Order, send ~~$75~~ $50 (plus postage and handling) by check or money order to:
Cardoza Publishing, P.O. Box 1500, Cooper Station, New York, NY 10276
